MEMORIES OF THE NIGHT:
A STUDY OF THE HOLOCAUST

By
Anita Meyer Meinbach and Miriam Klein Kassenoff

Photographs by Sharon Gurman Socol

FS-10179 Memories of the Night: A Study of the Holocaust
All rights reserved—Printed in the U.S.A.
Copyright © 1994 Frank Schaffer Publications, Inc.
23740 Hawthorne Blvd.
Torrance, CA 90505
ISBN 0-86734-777-5

DEDICATION

For my wonderful husband, Jay, and for my forever friend, Sharon Baron,
Both children of survivors—
Who will remember

And for my sons, Ken and David,
and for generations to come—
Who must remember

     AMM

For my loving parents, Maurice and Sara Klein, who saved me from the
Holocaust so that I could be a messenger. Their courage and love have
been a guiding force in my life.

     MKK

ACKNOWLEDGMENTS

Our thanks to those special people who shared their stories of courage and survival: Dina Abelson, Leon Bass, Ana Jinno, Vladka Meed, Abe Resnick.

For her support and helpful suggestions, our gratitude to Marcia Sabol, Museum Educator, U.S. Holocaust Museum, Washington, D.C.

We also wish to acknowledge the *Concord Monitor,* Concord, New Hampshire; *TOGETHER,* a publication of the American Gathering of Jewish Holocaust Survivors; and Facing History and Ourselves Resource Center for giving us permission to reprint portions of articles it has published.

A special thank-you to Sharon Socol, whose memorable photographs shed light on a dark subject.

Our deepest appreciation goes to Frank Schaffer, president of Frank Schaffer Publications, Inc., and to Jerry Aten, manager of Frank Schaffer's Middle School Division, for their commitment to this project and their belief in the importance of educating others about the lessons of the Holocaust.

Each of us has come to this work through our own avenues of interest and study of the Holocaust. Along the way there have been many special people who have helped us and to whom we individually wish to give thanks.

My interest in the Holocaust began when I was eight. Since then, my dedication and commitment to teaching others about the Holocaust has been nurtured by some very special people:

My parents Lucille and Alan Meyer who, by example, taught me about compassion, empathy, and love.

Rose and Max Fingerhut, survivors of the Holocaust, who first taught me about the courage of the human spirit.

My in-laws, Rae and Jack Meinbach, survivors of the Holocaust, who, after losing everything, came to this country and began again. Through their example, I am constantly reminded about the things in life that truly count.

Gene Greenzweig, the Chair of National Operations for the March of the Living, and all those at The Central Agency for Jewish Education connected with the March for selecting me to accompany our teens. The experience will remain with me always, the message never forgotten.

Dr. Liz Rothlein, Associate Dean of Education, University of Miami, who encouraged me to write this book—to turn a dream into reality.

AMM

I alone could not teach and be a messenger of the Holocaust without the support and love of others. I thank:

Dr. Barbara Carey, my supervisor and colleague, whose faith in me is ever-present and who inspires me to always reach beyond my grasp.

Octavio Visiedo, Superintendent of Dade County Public Schools, who has made it possible for me to continue my work with the Holocaust—he had the vision.

Dr. Michael Krop, for his constant support.

Judy Matz, for being there when needed.

Abe Resnick, who first discovered my abilities to teach about the Holocaust and helped make it possible.

Elaine Liftin and Evelyn Campbell, who opened the door to the possibilities.

Ben and Vladka Meed, who changed the course of my life's work.

Dr. Bill Renuart, principal, Miami Beach Senior High School, who always said, "Yes—do it."

Dr. Mary Johnson, for sharing her wealth of knowledge about the Holocaust.

My co-author, Anita Meinbach, who brought me into this project and without whom this book would not have been possible.

My friends—Annette, Lourdes, Susan, Katika, Dora, Penina, Alice, Gizzie, Karen, and Paula—who listened and listened...

And my family, Ted, Hank, Lisa, and, of course, my dear children, Debra and David.

MKK

Finally, this book is a tribute to the men, women, and children of the Holocaust. It is your voices that inspired this book. It is your memories that we hope to keep alive. Your courage and your spirit are our legacies.

TABLE OF CONTENTS

INTRODUCTION v
OVERVIEW vii
GETTING STARTED x
USING THIS BOOK xi

PART I: HISTORICAL PERSPECTIVES 1
Chapter 1: A World at War: The Social, Political, and Economic Climate of Europe 2
Chapter 2: All Through the Night: The Holocaust Years—1933–1945 10
Chapter 3: A New Dawn: Liberation, Rebirth, and the Nuremberg Trials 38
Chapter 4: Resistance and Rescue: The Heroes and Heroines of the Holocaust 47
Chapter 5: Prejudice, Stereotypes, and Scapegoats 63
Chapter 6: To Heal the World: Ethical Issues 68

PART II: THE LITERATURE OF THE HOLOCAUST 73

Individual and Group Responsibility:
    Terrible Things: An Allegory of the Holocaust 75
    Number the Stars 78

Resistance and Rescue:
    The Island on Bird Street 82
    Hannah Szenes: A Song of Light 86
    The Short Life of Sophie Scholl 90

Voices of the Holocaust:
    Daniel's Story 94
    The Devil's Arithmetic 98
    Alicia: My Story 102
    Anne Frank: The Diary of a Young Girl and *Anne Frank: Beyond the Diary* 106
    Night 111

Poetry, Art, and Photographs From the Holocaust:
    ...I Never Saw Another Butterfly 115
    The Children We Remember 119

PART III: THE HOLOCAUST: LESSONS FOR TODAY 122

APPENDICES: 133
    Time Line 134
    Glossary 137
    Resources: Bibliography of Books and Videos 141
        Holocaust Resource Centers 147

MEMORIES OF THE NIGHT:
A STUDY OF THE HOLOCAUST

INTRODUCTION

Nowhere in the world do the words of George Santayana become more prophetic than in the barracks of Auschwitz Concentration Camp, where they are surrounded by pictures and other artifacts to remind us of the 6,000,000 Jewish men, women, and children who died there and in other concentration camps throughout Germany and Poland. The words "Those who cannot remember the past are condemned to repeat it" becomes a haunting refrain, warning us of what happens when apathy replaces action, when tyranny replaces tolerance, and when hate replaces love.

This mass extermination, Hitler's systematic plan to destroy an entire people, has been termed the Holocaust. The Holocaust, one of the darkest chapters in the history of humankind, must be remembered to give meaning to the senseless slaughter of so many innocent victims. The lessons of the Holocaust must be taught so that children become aware of the devastating effects of prejudice. Through a study of the Holocaust, children learn about the importance of understanding and acceptance. And most importantly, through a study of the Holocaust, students learn the tremendous impact each individual can make—how one act of kindness multiplies in geometric proportions and how one person's courage can change the course of history.

Historically, the teaching of the Holocaust has been negligible. Most teachers lack the experience and understanding necessary to bring the Holocaust to life in the classroom, and, therefore, the teaching of the Holocaust has been delegated to one or two paragraphs in the history text. Will these paragraphs make students aware of the Holocaust? Yes. Will they cause students to feel sadness, anger, or disbelief? Possibly. Will they teach the lessons of the Holocaust; will they talk to students about tolerance, compassion, and the courage of the human spirit? Most assuredly not! To learn the lessons of the Holocaust, students need to meet those who were involved in it. They need to hear their stories, understand their reality, feel their despair, and celebrate their courage and dreams of survival.

Every two years, teens throughout the world take part in "The March of the Living." They meet in Poland and walk through the death camps of Auschwitz, Treblinka, and Majdanek. Of his experience, one student wrote

> Majdanek, the last of the camps we visited, affected me most. This camp was left exactly as it had been when the Nazis pulled out. We were allowed to physically touch what remained. There were three barracks filled with shoes, 800,000 pairs, 1,600,000 shoes in all. At one point I sat for ten minutes holding a shoe. I wondered who it had once belonged to, what he was like, and what he had accomplished. The shoe told me nothing. It was no different than any of the other shoes. What had taken this man a lifetime to accomplish was erased from the world in one fatal blow. All that remained to show he had existed was a name on a list, no different than 6,000,000 other names, and a pair of shoes every bit the same as 800,000 other pairs of shoes. I thought about the fact that one pair of shoes represented one human being, and I looked around to see the thousands of pairs surrounding me. I finally began to understand the enormity of the whole thing. Six million is just a number, abstract. It can't be touched or held. The shoes were concrete. They could be touched. They could be held. It was this that affected me the most...
> David Meinbach, June,1992

Obviously, we cannot take all of our students to Poland, and we cannot travel back in time. So, perhaps the best way to teach the Holocaust is through the voices of those who have lived it, through the words of those who are close to it.

Memories of the Night: A Study of the Holocaust is designed for teachers, to help them bring the lessons of the Holocaust to life. First-person accounts and the literature of the Holocaust form the basis for challenging, thought-provoking reflections and a variety of interdisciplinary activities that encourage students to connect the lessons of the Holocaust to the principles that will govern their own lives.

Holocaust study is a growing priority and mandated in many states across the country. While many question the relevance of studying the Holocaust, since "It happened a long time ago," and because "Other groups have also suffered," it is important to realize that the Holocaust is not being taught as something that happened to the Jewish people. It is being taught because it brings to the forefront profound universal truths of right and wrong, good over evil. You do not have to have a Jewish heart to listen to the message of the Holocaust; you have to have a human heart. Unless we stop the ethnic slurs, the prejudice, and the hatred, there will be another Holocaust. Unless we make the rest of the world stand up and take notice, *we will* be condemned to repeat the past. Already, we may be too late. Over 50 years after the Holocaust, genocide is being repeated in countries around the world, from Biafra to Bosnia.

In her diary, shortly before she and her family were discovered and deported to concentration camps, Anne Frank wrote, "It's really a wonder that I haven't dropped all my ideals, because they seem so absurd and impossible to carry out. Yet, I keep them, because, in spite of everything, I still believe that people are really good at heart." We as teachers have the opportunity, the responsibility, to guide a generation of youths to live up to this ideal.

OVERVIEW

Memories of the Night: A Study of the Holocaust is divided into three main sections which work together to bring the Holocaust and its message to students, as well as enable *all* students to relate the lessons of the Holocaust to their own lives and times.

PART I: HISTORICAL PERSPECTIVES

The six chapters in Part I provide students with information needed to understand the events leading to the Holocaust and allow them to experience the Holocaust through the voices of those who lived it. The chapters involve students in understanding the consequences of prejudice and apathy and charge them with the responsibility of ensuring "Never Again." As students explore the ethical issues involved in the Holocaust, it is hoped they will have the courage and determination to take a stand against evil in any form.

Each of the six chapters in Part I contains the following features:

- Historical Notes: a summary of information/events/people relevant to the chapter

- Through Their Eyes: stories of people directly affected by the events of the Holocaust. Each story is followed by several "Reaching Beyond" questions and activities that encourage students to react to the story and involve them in discussions of relevant issues. (Chapters 2–4)

- Reflections: questions to generate and guide discussion and writing that require students to reflect upon the historical notes, stories, and information gathered

- Extensions: a variety of interdisciplinary activities and research options to actively involve students in understanding and interpreting the lessons of the Holocaust

PART II: THE LITERATURE OF THE HOLOCAUST

The literature included and developed in Part II allows students to experience the Holocaust through the words, thoughts, and memories of its victims. The literature included extends the lessons and understandings of Part I in very personal ways. The selections present the sensitive nature of the Holocaust in ways to which students can relate. They are testimonials to the importance of understanding and accepting ourselves and others and of the profound need for courage, compassion, and kindness in the shadow of a world that often forgets.

For each literature selection in Part II, the following features are included:

- About the Author: information about the author and his/her involvement with the Holocaust

- Summary: a brief overview of the literary work to aid teachers and students in selecting the books they would like to read

- Vocabulary: definitions for terms related to the Holocaust that are generally unfamiliar to most readers

- Prereading Activity: an activity that establishes a purpose for reading and/or encourages students to connect background information with what they will be reading

- Questions and Answers: questions that guide students in their understanding of the material and encourage students to go back into the book

- Discussion Topics: suggestions that involve students in connecting what they have read with their own background knowledge and perspectives to make new observations and conclusions

- Writing Topics: suggestions that involve students in responding to the ideas and images about which they have read

- Extensions: interdisciplinary activities that allow students to pursue various ideas and concepts suggested by the literature

In selecting the literature to be included, several criteria were considered. The literature must:

- be historically correct and reflect all aspects of the Holocaust

- offer students the opportunity to reflect and draw their own conclusions

- serve as a reminder of the importance of standing up for what is right

- be widely regarded as outstanding, quality poetry or prose

- be easily accessible to the classroom teacher

- be varied and appropriate for a wide range of ability levels

Literature was also selected based on specific categories intrinsic to the study of the Holocaust. These categories are included as a guide to help teachers organize units of study:

Individual and Group Responsibility:
    Terrible Things (all levels—upper elementary through high school)
    Number the Stars (upper elementary and middle school grades)

Resistance and Rescue:
    The Island on Bird Street (all levels—upper elementary through high school)
    Hannah Szenes: A Song of Light (middle school and high school)
    The Short Life of Sophie Scholl (high school)

Voices of the Holocaust:
    Daniel's Story (upper elementary and middle school)
    The Devil's Arithmetic (historical fiction) (upper elementary and middle school)
    Alicia: My Story (middle school and high school)
    Anne Frank: The Diary of a Young Girl and *Anne Frank: Beyond the Diary* (middle school and high school)
    Night (middle school and high school)

Poetry, Art, and Photographs From the Holocaust:
    ...I Never Saw Another Butterfly... (all levels—upper elementary through high school)
    The Children We Remember (all levels—upper elementary through high school)

PART III: THE HOLOCAUST: LESSONS FOR TODAY

A variety of activities and reproducible activity sheets are provided in this section to allow students to apply the understanding and ideas they have gained through their involvement with the history and literature of the Holocaust. Activities will encourage independent and collaborative projects to enhance critical thinking skills and problem-solving skills, giving students the opportunity to extend their learning in relevant, meaningful ways. Activities, for example, range from ways to guide students in creating and responding in their own journals to the preparation of a Holocaust Remembrance Day as a culminating project.

APPENDICES:

The appendices include the following: time line; a glossary of terms relevant to the Holocaust; a comprehensive list of resources that teachers can use to further extend their teaching of the Holocaust. Resources include printed and non-printed materials as well as a list of agencies that offer various services to enhance the lessons of the Holocaust.

GETTING STARTED

Memories of the Night: A Study of the Holocaust explores many issues, including human suffering, the ability to survive under the most adverse circumstances, acts of heroism and resistance, and the manifestation of human dignity. The lessons and issues, however, extend far beyond the Holocaust to provide a framework for becoming empathetic, compassionate human beings with a set of values that include a responsibility for all humanity.

Before involving students in the material included in *Memories of the Night,* you may wish to introduce the unit with one of the videos suggested in the Resource Section of the Appendix, or you might prefer to introduce the unit with the following activity which helps to assess student knowledge, perceptions, and interest and gives students the opportunity to help establish goals for learning:

Initiating Activity:

1. Divide a large sheet of chart paper into these three columns: What I Know About the Holocaust; What I Want to Know About the Holocaust; What I Discovered About the Holocaust. Part III of *Memories of the Night* includes a similar chart. Distribute copies of the chart (page 125) to each student.

2. Ask students, "What do you know about the Holocaust?" Record their responses in the first column of the class chart. Next ask them, "What do you want to know about the Holocaust?" Record these responses in the second column.

3. Have students copy the responses in columns one and two of the class chart onto their own charts. As they become involved in learning about the Holocaust, encourage them to add to their own charts by listing new questions in the second column and recording the answers they find and insights they have gained in the third column.

4. At the end of the unit, have students discuss the information they learned and record this information under column three of the class chart. Compare the new information to that generated before they became involved in learning about the Holocaust. How have their ideas and perceptions changed?

USING THIS BOOK

Memories of the Night: A Study of the Holocaust is designed to complement any study of the Holocaust. The material can be adapted to almost any setting and can be used in a variety of ways. The following general ideas will help you use the book to it fullest advantage:

1. The Resource Section of the Appendix includes a comprehensive listing of books and media that will significantly enhance the lessons of the Holocaust. Try to obtain as many of these materials as possible so they can be used by students as they become involved with the various questions and activities suggested throughout the book.

2. The Time Line included in the Appendix can be enlarged or copied onto posterboard and displayed in the classroom for easy access.

3. The activities included throughout the book were purposely designed to allow for various group configurations. Students should be given the opportunity to work independently, in small groups, and in large groups, depending upon the activities selected.

4. Establish cooperative learning groups as students explore issues, discuss ideas, and pursue activities.

5. Many questions and activities are suggested throughout the book. Students should be given the opportunity to suggest their own questions and activities and to pursue them.

6. Provide time for students to share their writings and other projects.

7. To facilitate ease in using the book, the activities and questions included are addressed to the students. In this way they can simply be duplicated for student use or copied onto the chalkboard.

The following more specific suggestions are offered to help you optimize the use of the chapters, literature, and lessons included:

PART I:

1. The information included in Chapters 1–4 represents a chronology of the events of and leading to the Holocaust. Therefore, these chapters should be taken in order. Chapters 5 and 6 should be addressed after the first four chapters because they are based on an understanding of the Holocaust and the consequences of hatred and apathy.

2. The historical notes and stories included in these chapters can be read aloud by the teacher or duplicated to allow students to read them silently or with partners.

3. A wide variety of "Reflection" questions and "Extension" activities are offered so that students can be given a choice about which they would prefer to pursue.

PART II:

1. Twelve book units are developed for Part II. Each unit provides a summary which will help you and your students determine which book(s) to include in this unit of study. The grade levels of the books are listed in the "Overview" section.

2. You may wish to use one of the books as an introduction to the Holocaust or as a way of bringing the unit to a close. The books can also be read in conjunction with the study of the chapters in Part I.

3. You may wish to read one book aloud to your class while allowing small groups or individuals to read others, depending upon their interests and abilities. Whether students read the same book or different ones, they should be encouraged to get into "literature circles" to discuss the ideas suggested in the "Discussion Topics" section of each book unit and to share their responses to the "Writing Topics." If students read different books, they can first form literature circles with those who have read the same book, but ultimately the entire class should form a large literature circle that focuses on specific issues and concepts to determine how the different books address them and to aid students in forming their own conclusions and generalizations.

PART III:

1. All students should keep a journal to record their reactions and reflections as they take part in the study of the Holocaust. Often, journal writing is a catharsis, allowing them to sort out their feelings and express their emotions.

2. While students should be given the opportunity to select from the Individual and Collaborative Projects, one in particular is vital if the entire story of the Nazi atrocities is to be told— "Silent Voices." This activity remembers the other victims of the Nazis. Encourage students to become involved in the research of the Nazi murders of tens of thousands of non-Jews, including the Gypsies, the disabled, and the African-American prisoners of war.

3. In advance of the unit, try to make preparations for a class trip to see the movie *Schindler's List*. Discussion questions based on the movie are provided in this section.

4. The culminating activity, "Holocaust Remembrance Day," should be planned in conjunction with Holocaust Remembrance Week, usually held in April. Contact the U.S. Holocaust Museum (100 Raoul Wallenberg Place, S.W., Washington, D.C. 20004) for the specific date.

A final note: *Memories of the Night: A Study of the Holocaust* is a guide. Ultimately, the study of the Holocaust will raise more and more questions from your students. Use these questions to suggest new paths of learning that you and your students can follow. The lessons of the Holocaust are far-reaching; there are no limits to where they might lead.

PART 1
HISTORICAL PERSPECTIVES

View of tracks leading to Birkenau Death Camp, Poland

1

A World at War: The Social, Political, and Economic Climate of Europe

"If you want the present to be different from the past, study the past."

Baruch Spinoza

East Central Europe Prior to World War II

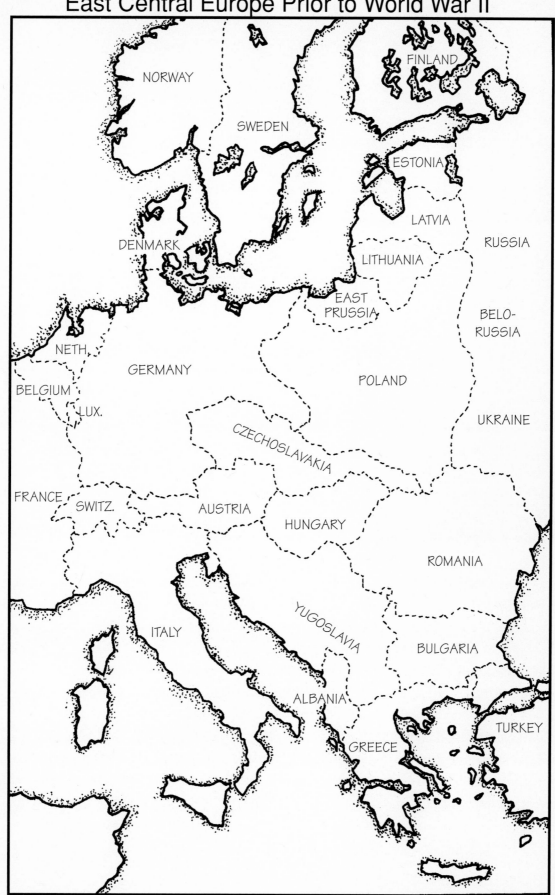

HISTORICAL NOTES

A WORLD AT WAR:
THE SOCIAL, POLITICAL, AND ECONOMIC CLIMATE OF EUROPE

The Holocaust is the term used to describe the Nazi program to annihilate the entire Jewish population of Europe. By the end of World War II, it was estimated that at least six million Jewish men, women, and children had perished as a result of the systematic extermination process developed by the Nazis. How did it all begin? How was it possible that the civilized society of Germany in the 1930s could be so quickly and easily seduced by Adolf Hitler and his followers to descend into the depths of hell to allow the Holocaust to happen?

Although anti-Semitism (hatred of Jews because of religious or cultural differences) goes back many centuries in Europe, for purposes of understanding this time period (1933–1945), one need only go back to the years immediately following World War I in Germany. Germany experienced political and economic crises after its humiliating defeat in World War I (1914–1918). The Treaty of Versailles was signed in 1919, and Germany was forced to pay high war reparations in addition to losing many of its territories and colonies. Factories were forced to shut down because of the destruction of Germany's foreign trade. The working classes suffered from poverty and unemployment. By 1932, more than 6,000,000 workers were unemployed. People at all levels, from the peasants to the middle class to the military, experienced severe hardships. The atmosphere was one of despair, making it difficult for democratic leadership. In fact, by 1933, the government had changed many times, always in economic and political crisis. The time was ripe for a dictatorship to arise—one that promised extreme measures to deliver the people from their misery.

In 1933, Adolf Hitler was appointed Chancellor of Germany. A strong, charismatic leader, Hitler soon overthrew the government's constitution and created a dictatorship which permitted only one party—the Nazi Party. He had already formed the National Socialist German Workers' Party—the Nazi party—in 1919. Nazism and its ideology responded to the deep problems in Germany. Besides the support Hitler had from the military on ideas of discipline, order, and conquest, Hitler's promise of social reform attracted the support of the masses. By 1929, the Nazi Party had many thousands of members. Once Hitler and the Nazi Party were in power, they took over the press, the radio, and the school system. In a short time, a totalitarian state was established and the Gestapo, the state police, was organized to monitor and stamp out any opposition. Concentration camps were set up for anyone opposing Nazism.

The Jewish people became the obsession of the Nazi party and prime target for persecution. The question "Why the Jews?" is frequently asked. There were many reasons. Hitler had a grand scheme for a perfect nation of pure people. In Germany, the Jewish people, despite their presence there for generations, were considered "a foreign element." It was, according to Hitler, the Jews who were keeping the "Fatherland" (Germany) impure. In addition, the Jewish people were considered too liberal in their ideology, embracing freedoms of religion, speech, and thought, ideals for which Hitler had no regard. The Jewish community, by 1930, had unified into such strength through their activities that they held leadership positions in political parties and trade unions. Jews had increased their cultural activity, establishing special Hebrew school systems and Zionist Youth Movements. They were the leading scholars at the universities; they were outstanding artists and musicians; they were respected doctors, lawyers, and merchants. Yet, despite the contributions of the Jewish community, the masses resented their successes and blamed the Jews for the economic problems that plagued the land. Jews, then, were targets for persecution because they were considered different. They were a minority. They practiced their own religion and had many of their own traditions which were different from those of other religions. They were successful.

It was easy for Hitler to plant the seeds of distrust, doubt, and fear of the Jew since prejudice and anti-Semitism had existed in Europe for almost 2,000 years. As early as 1912, posters and cartoons could be found depicting the Jewish people as a deadly snake strangling the country, with sums of money written on its back to symbolize Jewish capitalism.

The Jewish people became a convenient and perfect scapegoat (person or group blamed for the mistakes, problems, or crimes of others), a phenomenon on which dictatorships thrive. Hitler began a brilliant, comprehensive propaganda campaign to turn people against their Jewish friends and neighbors. He developed a Nazi ideology that professed that the Jews were a demonic, destructive race of people who had to be completely destroyed. All Jews. No exceptions.

A method of systematic persecution was begun. Little by little, the Jewish people lost their rights. The Nuremberg Laws, passed in 1935, made racism legal, giving Jews inferior status and even stripping them of their German citizenship. These laws were designed to isolate the Jews socially and politically. The nightmare had begun.

Umschlagplatz; the platform of the train station from which the Jews of the Warsaw Ghetto were transported to Auschwitz and other concentration camps. The soldier evokes images of the Nazi guards.

A WORLD AT WAR:
THE SOCIAL, POLITICAL, AND
ECONOMIC CLIMATE OF EUROPE

REFLECTIONS

1. How did the results of World War I pave the way for German aggression in World War II?

2. What relationship can you find between economic, social, and political conditions and the rise of dictators?

3. What effect did the Nuremburg Laws have upon the way in which German citizens viewed their Jewish neighbors? How could a law have such an impact upon the public, changing perceptions and attitudes?

4. Why did Hitler's plan to eliminate the Jews gain such wide acceptance throughout most of Europe?

5. What elements combined to make it possible for a Holocaust to take place? Based on your knowledge of these elements, what can be done to prevent another Holocaust?

EXTENSIONS

1. Research the Treaty of Versailles. With a group of other students, analyze the different terms of the treaty and their effect on German economy, society, and politics, as well as on neighboring countries. Create a five-minute presentation that briefly explains three of the treaty's terms and their implications.

2. Individually, in small groups, or as a class, complete the chart on the following page to indicate the political, economic, and social conditions that gave rise to a dictatorship in post-World War I Germany. Discuss which of these conditions you believe to be the most significant and be prepared to explain your answer.

3. Imagine that you are a non-Jewish German citizen who has just seen the Nuremburg Laws posted for the first time. With another student, create and present a conversation between you and a Jewish friend in which you attempt to explain the laws and your friend reacts to them. (Chapter 2 includes a copy of the Nuremburg Laws.)

4. Imagine that you and your classmates are foreign correspondents in Germany. You are working together to send a newspaper to the United States that details the events in Germany from January 30, 1933, when Hitler became Chancellor, to September 3, 1939, the official date of the outbreak of World War II. Using the timeline provided on pages 134–136, select and research a specific event you find especially significant or interesting. Write a news column to describe it. Put your columns together with others written by classmates to create your paper. Be certain to include headlines, photographs, pictures, and captions.

5. Create a large floor map of Europe before World War II. Use it throughout your study of the Holocaust. Label cities and areas of special importance to the study of the Holocaust and label the sites of significant events.

THE RISE OF A DICTATORSHIP

POLITICAL CONDITIONS	ECONOMIC CONDITIONS	SOCIAL CONDITIONS

CHAPTER 2

All Through the Night: The Holocaust Years 1933–1945

"I remember the fear, the clear knowledge that we could be taken to the camps at any time or simply shot, only for being Jews."

Ana Jinno
child survivor from
Kosicé, Czechoslovakia

The Concentration Camps

Map labels:
NORWAY, SWEDEN, FINLAND, ESTONIA, • Vaivara, • Klooga, LATVIA, LITHUANIA, DENMARK, EAST PRUSSIA, • Stutthof, **Treblinka**, • Neuengamme, • Bergen-Belsen, • Ravensbrück, POLAND, **Sobibor**, NETH., • Mittelbau Dora, • Sachsenhausen, **Chelmno**, **Majdanek**, BELGIUM, • Buchenwald, • Gross Rosen, **Auschwitz**, U.S.S.R., LUX., GERMANY, • Flossenberg, CZECHOSLAVAKIA, • Plaszow, **Belzec**, • Natzweiler, • Dachau, FRANCE, SWITZ., • Mauthausen, AUSTRIA, HUNGARY, ROMANIA, • Gospic, Jasenovac •, YUGOSLAVIA, • Sajmiste, BULGARIA, ITALY, ALBANIA, TURKEY, GREECE

Auschwitz concentration camp in which more than 2 million people were murdered between 1941 and 1944, including Jews, Gypsies, and Soviet prisoners-of-war.

▬ Camps set up solely for the murder of Jews.

● Other camps in which Jews and non-Jews were put to forced labor, starved, tortured, and murdered in conditions of the worst imaginable cruelty.

HISTORICAL NOTES

ALL THROUGH THE NIGHT: THE HOLOCAUST YEARS—1933-1945

Once Hitler established power in 1933, conditions for the Jewish people became more and more impossible. The Nuremberg Laws handed down in 1935 decreed that only persons of "German blood" (Aryans) could be citizens of Germany, while persons of "impure blood" (non-Aryans) were of inferior status and were not citizens. The following are the "Nuremberg Law for the Protection of German Blood and German Honor" and the "First Regulation of the Reich Citizenship Law."

(Note to teachers: You may find sections of the Nuremberg Laws too explicit for your students. Read them carefully before sharing them with your class and use your best discretion as to which sections should be shared.)

NUREMBERG LAW FOR THE PROTECTION OF
GERMAN BLOOD AND GERMAN HONOR,
SEPTEMBER 15, 1935

Law for the Protection of German Blood and German Honor
September 15, 1935

Moved by the understanding that purity of the German Blood is the essential condition for the continued existence of the German people, and inspired by the inflexible determination to ensure the existence of the German Nation for all time, the Reichstag has unanimously adopted the following Law, which is promulgated herewith:

§ 1

1) Marriages between Jews and subjects of the state of German or related blood are forbidden. Marriages nevertheless concluded are invalid, even if concluded abroad to circumvent this law.
2) Annulment proceedings can be initiated only by the State Prosecutor.

§ 2

Extramarital intercourse between Jews and subjects of the state of German or related blood is forbidden.

§ 3

Jews may not employ in their households female subjects of the state of German or related blood who are under 45 years old.

§ 4

1) Jews are forbidden to fly the Reich or National flag or to display the Reich colors.

2) They are, on the other hand, permitted to display the Jewish colors. The exercise of this right is protected by the State.

§ 1) Any person who violates the prohibition under § 1 will be punished by a prison sentence with hard labor. 2) A male who violates the prohibition under § 2 will be punished with a prison sentence with or without hard labor. 3) Any person violating the provisions under § § 3 or 4 will be punished with a prison sentence of up to one year and a fine, or with one or the other of these penalties.

The Reich Minister of the Interior, in coordination with the Deputy of the Führer and the Reich Minister of Justice, will issue the Legal and Administrative regulations required to implement and complete this Law.

The Law takes effect on the day following promulgations except for § 3, which goes into force on January 1, 1936.

Nuremberg, September 15, 1935 at the Reich Party Congress of Freedom

The Führer and Reich Chancellor
Adolf Hitler
The Reich Minister of the Interior
Frick
The Reich Minister of Justice
Dr. Gürtner
The Deputy of the Führer
R. Hess

Reichsgesetzblatt, I, *1935, pp.* 1146-1147.

Source: Arad, Y. et al, Eds. *Documents on the Holocaust:* Yad Vashem: KTAV Publishing House, 1981.

First Regulation to the Reich Citizenship Law
November 14, 1935

1) A Jew cannot be a Reich citizen. He has no voting rights in political matters; he cannot occupy a public office.
2) Jewish officials will retire as of December 31, 1935...

1) A Jew is a person descended from at least three grandparents who are full Jews by race...
2) A *Mischling* who is a subject of the state is also considered a Jew if he is descended from two full Jewish grandparents
   a) who was a member of the Jewish Religious Community at the time of the promulgation of this Law, or was admitted to it subsequently;
   b) who was married to a Jew at the time of the promulgation of this Law, or subsequently married to a Jew;
   c) who was born from a marriage with a Jew in accordance with paragraph 1, contracted subsequently to the promulgation of the Law for the Protection of German Blood and German Honor of September 15, 1935 *(Reichsgesetzblatt,* I, p. 1146);
   d) who was born as the result of extramarital intercourse with a Jew in accordance with Paragraph 1, and was born illegitimately after July 31, 1936...

Source: Arad, Y. et al, Eds. *Documents on the Holocaust:* Yad Vashem: KTAV Publishing House, 1981.

The result of these laws was that Jews were no longer free to keep their jobs or property. Racism and anti-Semitism were legitimized. In this environment of hate, approximately 80,000 German Jews left their homes. By 1938, as Nazi anti-Jewish policy became more aggressive, many thousands of German Jews had fled.

On the night of November 9, 1938, the Nazis unleashed their "orgy of devastation." It was forever to be known in the history of the Holocaust as *Kristallnacht,* the "Night of Broken Glass." Jewish homes, shops, and businesses were looted and destroyed. The Nazis burned synagogues and arrested thousands of Jews, killing hundreds more. The shattered glass that littered the streets gave that night of horrors its name. With the destruction came the grim reality of what life had become for the Jewish people and a foreshadowing of the horror yet to come. Soon after Kristallnacht, thousands of Jews were arrested and taken to already established concentration camps created for political dissidents. The next step was to expel Jews from their homes, isolate them in ghettos, and finally confine them to prison and labor camps.

By 1939, not only were Jews restricted, but Jehovah's Witnesses were also arrested in Germany, as were an estimated 250,000 Gypsies, who were later sent to concentration camps. Hitler further decreed that those who were incurably sick be put to death, so euthanasia centers were opened. All this was done in the name of purifying Germany from undesirables.

In September, 1939, the German army invaded Poland and millions of Jews found themselves under Nazi rule. In each country that the Germans ultimately conquered, Hitler spread his Nazi propaganda of hate against the Jews. Jews were forced to wear the yellow Star of David, and were forcibly removed from their homes and placed in special areas called "ghettos." The ghettos were overcrowded and Jews there suffered from hunger and disease. The largest ghetto was the Warsaw Ghetto in Poland, which at one time held 400,000 people in an area of approximately 3.5 square miles.

By 1940, a priority of the Nazi government was to cleanse Europe of all Jews. The first stage of the annihilation or extermination of the Jews began with the Special Action Groups, or *Einsatzgruppen*. These were specially trained Nazi commandos who were mobile firing squads. They would arrive in a city, order all Jews to gather at a certain place such as the town square, strip them of all their valuables, shoot them, and throw their corpses into ditches. Often the Jews were made to dig the ditches and were then lined up along the edge so that the force of the bullets would cause them to fall in. Other times, mobile killing vans were used. These trucks had specially built pipe exhaust fumes and Jews were gassed to death inside the vans.

These methods, however, were not efficient enough—the Nazis wanted a faster, easier way to annihilate the Jewish people. The following page contains a memo the Nazi leader Hermann Göring wrote to the SS Gruppenführer Heydrich asking him to prepare a plan for the "Final Solution of the Jewish Problem."

GÖRING ORDERS HEYDRICH TO PREPARE A PLAN
FOR THE "FINAL SOLUTION OF THE JEWISH PROBLEM,"
JULY 31, 1941

To the Chief of the Security Police and the SD, *SS Gruppenführer*
Heydrich, Berlin

In completion of the task which was entrusted to you in the Edict dated
January 24, 1939, of solving the Jewish question by means of emigration
or evacuation in the most convenient way possible, given the present
conditions, I herewith charge you with making all necessary
preparations with regard to organizational, practical and financial
aspects for an overall solution *(Gesamtlösung)* of the Jewish question in
the German sphere of influence in Europe.
Insofar as the competencies of other central organizations are affected,
these are to be involved.
I further charge you with submitting to me promptly an overall plan of
the preliminary organizational, practical and financial measures for the
execution of the intended final solution *(Endlösung)* of the Jewish
question.

      Göring

Source: Arad, Y. et al., Eds. *Documents on the Holocaust:* Yad Vashem:
KTAV Publishing House, 1981.

By the year 1940, Germany occupied Denmark, Norway, Belgium, France, Poland, and
Czechoslovakia; the Germans could literally plan a mass murder of Jews from any of these
countries. They chose Poland for the six major death camps—Sobibor, Treblinka, Auschwitz-
Birkenau, Belzec, Majdanek, and Chelmno—since most of the Jews of Eastern Europe were
concentrated there and the land was suitable, with its many miles of forests, to hide secret operations
(see map, page 11). In addition, the Nazis had little concern that the majority of the people in rural
Poland witnessing these exterminations would do anything to stop them.

*Arbeit Macht Frei; German for "Work Makes You Free." This sign, ironic in its
message, hung over the entrance of Auschwitz Death Camp, Poland.*

In 1942, at the Wannsee Conference, the decision was made to implement the "Final Solution to the Jewish Question"—mass extermination. The following is an extract from written evidence of Rudolf Höss, Commander of the Auschwitz Extermination Camp, detailing the final solution.

**EXTRACT FROM WRITTEN EVIDENCE OF RUDOLF HÖSS,
COMMANDER OF THE AUSCHWITZ
EXTERMINATION CAMP**

In the summer of 1941, I cannot remember the exact date, I was suddenly summoned to the *Reichsführer SS,* directly by his adjutant's office. Contrary to his usual custom, Himmler received me without his adjutant being present and said in effect:
"The Führer has ordered that the Jewish question be solved once and for all and that we, the SS, are to implement that order.

The existing extermination centers in the East are not in a position to carry out the large *Aktionen* which are anticipated. I have therefore earmarked Auschwitz for this purpose, both because of its good position as regards communications and because the area can easily be isolated and camouflaged. At first I thought of calling in a senior SS officer for this job, but I changed my mind in order to avoid difficulties concerning the terms of reference. I have now decided to entrust this task to you. It is difficult and onerous and calls for complete devotion notwithstanding the difficulties that may arise. You will learn further details from Sturmbannführer Eichmann of the Reich Security Main Office who will call on you in the immediate future.

The departments concerned will be notified by me in due course. You will treat this order as absolutely secret, even from your superiors. After your talk with Eichmann you will immediately forward to me the plans for the projected installations.

The Jews are the sworn enemies of the German people and must be eradicated. Every Jew that we can lay our hands on is to be destroyed now during the war, without exception. If we cannot now obliterate the biological basis of Jewry, the Jews will one day destroy the German people."

On receiving these grave instructions, I returned forthwith to Auschwitz, without reporting to my superior at Oranienburg.

Shortly afterwards Eichmann came to Auschwitz and disclosed to me the plans for the operations as they affected the various countries concerned. I cannot remember the exact order in which they were to take place. First was to come the eastern part of Upper Silesia and the neighboring parts of Polish territory under German rule, then, depending on the situation, simultaneously Jews from Germany and Czechoslovakia, and finally the Jews from the West: France, Belgium and Holland. He also told me the approximate number of transports that might be expected, but I can no longer remember these.

Source: Arad, Y. et al, Eds. *Documents on the Holocaust:* Yad Vashem: KTAV Publishing House, 1981.

Jews throughout Europe were rounded up from the various ghettos and told they were going to be taken "to the east" to work. To further enhance the lie, the Jewish people were told they could take one bag of valuables and belongings to help them with their resettlement. The Jews were then shoved into railroad cattle cars and transported for days without room to move and without food and water.

Once they arrived in the camps, "selections" were made by the Nazis. Strong prisoners went one way to be kept for labor, while most women and children, along with the weak and elderly, were sent in another direction, which ultimately led to the gas chambers. But first, they were stripped and their heads were shaved. Then they were sent to the showers, but instead of water emerging, a poisonous gas (Zyklon-B) was released. Victims screamed and clawed at the cement doors that held them, trying to escape—but there was no escape and their bodies were tossed into crematoriums.

Life in the camps was a slower form of death. Victims were routinely beaten, tortured, and starved. Clothing was thin and could not protect them from the bitter cold. Medical experiments were perfomed on many, often without anesthesia. Women were raped by their captors and forced to withstand unbelievable humiliation. Disease was rampant. It was a living hell.

Bodies of Jewish men, women, and children were thrown into the ovens of crematoriums in the death camps.

*above: Barracks at Auschwitz Death Camp were as bleak as the lives of the prisoners. **left:** Headquarters of SS at Auschwitz Death Camp*

By the end of the war, over 6,000,000 Jewish men, women, and children had been killed.

NUMBERS OF JEWISH PEOPLE KILLED IN DIFFERENT COUNTRIES

Poland	3,000,000	Yugoslavia	67,000
The Soviet Union	1,000,000	Austria	65,000
Romania	365,000	Belgium	24,000
Hungary	305,000	Italy	8,000
Czechoslovakia	270,000	Estonia	1,000
Germany	160,000	Norway	728
Lithuania	135,000	Luxembourg	700
The Netherlands	106,000	Libya	562
France	83,000	Albania	200
Latvia	80,000	Denmark	77
Greece	71,300	Finland	11

source: *Judaica Encyclopedia,* Vol. 8, page 889.

Many people today ask, "Where was the rest of the world?" and "Why didn't the Jews resist?" It must be understood that, without question, the Jews were abandoned by the rest of the world. The events involving the ship *St. Louis* serve as a perfect example. In 1938, the Nazis were still anxious to rid Germany of Jews so they encouraged shipping lines to transport the Jews. The Hamburg-American Line prepared a ship called the *St. Louis*, bound for Cuba, and sold about 900 visas to German Jews. When the ship entered port in Cuba, the landing certificates were claimed to be illegal by the Cuban Government. The whole world was watching as the *St. Louis,* full of German immigrants, anxiously awaited permission to disembark its passengers. Ultimately, no permission was granted and the *St. Louis* sailed to the United States, hugging the shoreline of Florida. But, because the United States had strict immigration policies concerning Jewish refugees, the ship was not allowed to land in the United States either.

Finally, the ship, with no country willing to grant its passengers refuge, returned to Germany, where more than half of the passengers met their death. The United States and the other nations had turned their backs on the cries of humanity. Why? Once more, anti-Semitism had reared its ugly head and the fear of taking in so many refugees was more than any one country wished to handle.

The answer to the second question, "Why didn't the Jews resist?" is more complicated, for there are many reasons. First, the Jews were not militarily prepared. They were ordinary citizens like you and me, living ordinary lives, when they were suddenly taken from their homes by force, uninformed and unarmed. Second, once the Jews were in ghettos, they were starved to death and became riddled with disease. They were physically and spiritually weakened. Daily existence depended on finding food. Third, even when news of the death camps reached their ears, the Jewish people could not imagine that such horror could be true. They believed that the war would soon end and that life would become as it was—if only they could survive. Finally, even before the full impact of the Nazi "Final Solution" became evident, there were instances of resistance; but rebellion led to reprisals, and one Jew rebelling often meant death for hundreds more. Yet, despite all these reasons, there were forms of spiritual and physical resistance—the Jews did fight back (see Chapter 4: Resistance and Rescue); but, in the end, they were no match for the huge Nazi war machine.

And so, the Holocaust, the carefully planned and systematic annihilation of a people, brought unimaginable suffering. While reading about the Holocaust is difficult, it is vital. If we are to learn anything from the past, the Holocaust must be remembered. To make any sense of this tragedy, the Holocaust must be remembered. To give meaning to the millions of lives that were cut short, the Holocaust must be remembered.

The Nazis collected all personal possessions of the Jewish people. Eventually, after the "Final Solution" had been carried out, they planned to create a museum filled with the possessions of an extinct culture.

THROUGH THEIR EYES
Vladka Meed's Personal Recollections of the Warsaw Ghetto Uprising

Vladka Meed is a respected authority and leader in the training of Holocaust educators throughout the United States. Having been one of the leaders of the Warsaw Ghetto Uprising, she shares her knowledge and experience through the teacher training program she founded through the American Gathering of Jewish Holocaust Survivors.

Fifty years have passed. Mila 18, the house which served as the headquarters of the Warsaw Ghetto Fighters, is no more. A small patch of grass, a few flowers during the summer time and a big, lonely rock with faded lines mark the place. A short distance away stands the well-known ghetto monument, a granite block with a chiseled scene of ghetto fighters. Two tragic reminders of an isolated heroic defiance of the Warsaw Ghetto Uprising.

Beyond the lonely symbols, I can still see the flames from the burning houses leaping over the ghetto walls and through the clouds of thick smoke, I can still hear the sounds of explosions and the firing of Jewish guns. In its glare, I see my people from Warsaw and from other ghettos and towns. I see their suffering, their struggle, their resistance during all the years of the Nazi occupation.

Their resistance took on different forms at different times. I recall the crowded Warsaw Ghetto streets with starving people. Children, swollen from hunger. Corpses lying unclaimed on the sidewalks. I remember my neighbor standing in the doorway of the building, watching out for approaching Germans, while upstairs her daughter held secret classes for children. I recall the illegal schools in the ghetto, the secret libraries, clandestine synagogues, underground cultural events, political youth groups with their activities and publications. Alongside the horrible suffering, terror and death, there was a pulsating life in the ghettos—a life filled with meaning, with dignity and even with hope. This was the essence of resistance with a will to survive and a spirit that refused to be crushed. This was the soil in which the seeds of our later form of organized armed resistance took hold.

Then came "the Final Solution." The carefully coordinated Nazi machinery of mass murder went into operation. Suddenly, streets and homes were surrounded by armed soldiers, police, Ukrainians and fast, fast, amid blows and shots, our people were forced to line up. I remember them, the old, the young, the little ones, filled with fear of the unknown, walking silently under pointed rifles, to the trains. As their footsteps echo in my mind, I can still hear their unuttered outcry to the world which let this happen. Yet—even then, many still had the futile hope, that deportation was nothing more than the Germans had claimed—resettlement in the East.

How could our people, who for generations believed and cherished human values, imagine such evil as that of an enemy who planned our total destruction. It took time until the ghetto started to believe the horrible truth of gas chambers, a truth brought back by victims who somehow escaped death.

Then came the last stage of resistance, the determination to die fighting. The coordinated Jewish Fighters Organization—ZOB—was formed. Its core was our remaining youth in the ghetto. Over 500 idealistic, determined young people of prewar political groups were organized into 22 units. Other independent fighting groups were also formed.

I was given the task to get out of the ghetto, live among the Poles and, together with a few others, try to obtain arms for the Fighters Organization. How to get arms was our main concern. The ghetto had no arms. We turned to the outside world, to the Polish Underground—but the response was pitiful. We had to find our own way. I remember the breakthrough, when Michel Klepfish, our so-called armament engineer, learned to make our first homemade Molotov cocktail and, together, we tested it in the large furnace of a factory outside the ghetto wall—and it worked.

With mounting excitement, we smuggled chemicals and dynamite into the ghetto. Primitive factories were set up in attics. On my missions to the ghetto, I could hear the sounds of hammering. Jews were building bunkers, hiding places. Bakers secretly supplied bread to our units. Money, jewelry were collected for armaments. "Resist! Don't let yourself be taken away," was the call.

"I no longer have any authority in the ghetto," Mark Lichtenbaum, the head of the appointed Jewish Council, admitted to the Nazis when he was ordered to supervise further deportation. The Fighters Organization expressed the will and the feelings of the remaining 50,000 Warsaw Ghetto Jews.

The hour struck on Passover, Easter, April 19, 1943. At 2 a.m., the guard of the Fighters Organization noticed the movement of new German troops near the ghetto walls. The whole ghetto was immediately alerted. Fighters took up their positions; others were ordered to the prepared bunkers and hiding places. When German soldiers marched into the ghetto to make it "Judenrein," they found the streets empty. Suddenly, at certain intersections, they came under fire. From buildings, from windows, from rooftops, the Jews were shooting. The enemy withdrew.

The Germans set up artillery around the ghetto wall, and from there they systematically bombarded the ghetto houses. Still the ghetto did not yield. One of our units, at the entrance of the brush-makers factory, wailed with anticipation for the approaching enemy. When the first soldiers started to enter, a silent signal from the commander, and a moment later, a loud explosion. It was one of the four mines which went off. We were so poorly equipped. Inexperienced, untrained civilians against a well-oiled military machine, the Wermacht, fully armed with tanks, artillery and planes.

Block after block, house after house, the Germans set on fire. The fire that swept into the ghetto turned night into day. The flames, the heat, the suffocating smoke, drove people from their hiding places. Men, women, children, jumped out of windows and ran through burning ruins, looking for a place where they could breathe. But, where could they go, when everything around them was burning? And in the midst of this flaming hell, fighting went on, until the ghetto was reduced to charred rubble.

General Jurgen Stroop, who destroyed the Warsaw Ghetto, stated in an official report that on May 16, he ordered the remaining synagogue on Tlomacka Street to be blown up as a sign of his victory over the fighting ghetto, after four weeks of struggle. We know, of course, that after that time, the ghetto was unable to continue organized resistance, since the majority of our military organization had been killed. Mordechai Anielewicz, leader of the uprising, and his staff were gassed at the headquarters at Mila 18. Many others were burned to death. But for many weeks afterwards, shots from the ghetto were still heard.

Our people, who put so much hope in the free world, were entirely alone, forsaken in their last, final hours. Only one year later, I was at the uprising of Polish Warsaw. I remember, at that time, the planes flying over the city, dropping arms and medical supplies to the Polish fighters. But when we fought, the skies over the ghetto were empty.

In the months afterwards, we learned of organized Jewish Uprisings in other ghettos and camps, of Jewish partisans fighting in the forests. Our people resisted the enemy in all possible ways and forms until the end.

We now stand at a distance from the shattering times in the ghetto of Warsaw and we look back and remember. The story of the Warsaw Ghetto Uprising, doomed from the start, must remain a ringing warning, and an inspiration to all people, in all times.

Reprinted with permission from *TOGETHER,* June 1993, and from

---

Reaching Beyond

1. Information on organized resistance against the Nazis is frequently overlooked in history books. Why is it important that we have eye-witness information such as Vladka's that there was organized resistance?

2. Vladka recalls that "alongside the horrible suffering, terror and death, there was a pulsating life in the ghettos—a life filled with meaning, with dignity and even with hope. This was the essence of resistance." Discuss this quote. What does she mean by the phrase "the essence of resistance?"

3. Why couldn't the Jewish people in the ghetto believe the horrible truths they were beginning to hear about the gas chambers from victims who had somehow escaped?

4. Describe the tasks and obstacles the ZOB (Jewish Fighters Organization) had to overcome to plan the Warsaw Ghetto Uprising? What was Vladka's specific task?

5. People frequently ask, "Why didn't the Jews fight back?" Now that you have heard Vladka's story, how would you respond to that question?

6. Vladka Meed and her husband, Benjamin Meed, both survived the Holocaust. They now head the American Gathering of Survivors of the Jewish Holocaust and are leading founders of the U.S. Holocaust Museum in Washington, D.C. Try to arrange a trip to this incredible museum, which is a testimonial to the millions who died, a reminder that we have not forgotten, a promise of "Never Again."

THROUGH THEIR EYES

ABE'S STORY

Abe Resnick survived the Holocaust to become one of South Florida's most respected leaders. The following describes portions of his life during the nightmare years, including the years he spent in the Kovno Ghetto.

Abraham Resnickowitz was born in 1924, in Rokishki, Lithuania, a town of 7,000 citizens—50 percent of whom were Jewish. Life in Rokishki before World War II was good. Abe's family, including his father, a governmental insurance inspector, his mother, and two younger sisters, enjoyed an active social life. Rokishki was a quiet, peaceful town, paved with cobblestone streets. A small lake was situated in the middle of the town, surrounded by shade trees. Once a week the town attracted people from neighboring villages to its outdoor market, which sold delicious foods and beautiful clothing.

As a young teen-age boy, Abe had many friends. Often, they went on outings, riding their bikes from the town into the countryside. There they would meet other friends, sit around campfires singing songs and sharing their future plans. They could not know then that most of their plans would never come true. They could not know then that the peace and serenity of their world would soon erupt into chaos and destruction.

When it was time for formal education, Abe was sent to the Gymnasium, a private institute of higher learning, located in Lithuania's capital city, Kovno. The years there were good to Abe. He studied hard, focusing on medicine, but also led an active life, filled with cultural pursuits. In 1941, after completing eight years at the Gymnasium, he was ready to apply to a university in Italy to study medicine. Before he had the opportunity to attend medical school, before he even had the opportunity to visit with his parents at the end of the school year, the Nazis attacked Russia, including Lithuania. Kovno was bombed. Abe tried to flee, hoping he could reach home. He was only 150 miles away, but it might as well have been thousands of miles. The roads were shelled and surrounded by the Nazi Army. Abe had no recourse but to return to his apartment in Kovno, where his grandmother, aunt, and uncle also lived.

The Nazis immediately began their campaign of cruelty against the Jews, aided by Nazi sympathizers and local Lithuanian anti-Semites. Women were raped. Children were shot on sight. Within a few weeks, the Nazis formed a small ghetto in an area of about two square miles to hold between 20,000 and 25,000 Jews. Abe, his grandmother, uncle, and aunt were forced into the Kovno Ghetto. Soon after the family was imprisoned in the ghetto, the Nazis announced they needed 500 educated people for a special assignment with a promised reward of extra food. Abe tried to volunteer, but was too late, as the quota was quickly filled. Disappointed at a missed opportunity, Abe was later to discover that the special assignment was execution. The Nazis had wanted to rid the ghetto of its most educated prisoners, those that might prove to be the most difficult to control. Abe had escaped death, for the first time.

The Nazis demanded that all Jews in the Kovno Ghetto relinquish all their valuables. If any valuables were found on anyone at anytime, all members of that person's family were hanged. To prove they meant business, the Nazis hanged an innocent Jew in the center of the ghetto. Abe was forced to watch. These and other images of terror and brutality were to become the memories of childhood that would never leave him. Over 50 years later, these memories still haunt Abe.

Four months after the horror began, in October 1941, the Nazis began separating people—some were motioned to the left, others to the right. Abe realized that the older and weaker people were on one side, while the younger and stronger were ordered to the other. He quickly grabbed his grandmother and pushed her to the side he was on. For a time, he was able to save her.

By now, Abe had heard rumors that most of the Jews in the small towns like Rokishki, his home, were being shot and buried in ditches they had been forced to dig. Witnesses from other ghettos who were transported to the Kovno Ghetto verified these rumors, and Abe heard the devastating news that his entire family had perished—his mother, his father, his sisters. He would never again see their faces. He was 17. He felt completely alone.

Abe remained in the Kovno Ghetto until May 1944. He worked hard in forced labor brigades with little food to sustain him. His only goal was self-preservation—to survive—hour by hour, day by day. At this time, only 7,000 of the original 38,000 Jews were still living in the ghetto; the rest had either died due to the inhumane conditions in the ghetto or had been transported to death camps. Now, the Nazis began liquidating the ghetto to rid it of the remaining few, because the Russian armies were approaching. Abe and a few of his comrades knew they had to escape. After careful planning, they eluded the guards and hid in an abandoned house in the ghetto. When night fell, they cut through the barbed wire surrounding the ghetto, and moved quickly in the darkness of the woods. In the morning, they made their way to a nearby village. They were immediately spotted and one of his group was killed by the local militia. Abe and three companions escaped—another reprieve from death.

Abe and his friends decided it would be safer if they moved in different directions. Once they split up, Abe never saw nor heard of any of the others again. It was not long before Abe found a group of partisans in Lithuania and joined their efforts for a short period of time. A few months later, the Russian Army liberated Kovno and Abe then joined the Russian Army, hoping to avenge the death of his family by fighting against the Nazis. Abe became an interpreter for the Russians and subsequently was promoted to a lieutenant in the Russian Army. He participated in liberating Berlin and the concentration camp of Sachsenhausen. Years later he would say that this was one of the momentous occasions in his life.

Abe remained with the Russian Army until 1947. When he saw the opportunity to escape, he made his way to France and eventually immigrated to Cuba, where he knew a few of his relatives lived. Abe spent 13 productive, happy years in Havana, Cuba. He was able to find some of his relatives; he married, raised two sons, and became a prominent business and community leader.

But his security was short-lived. In 1959, with Fidel Castro's rise to power as the head of a Communist regime in Cuba, Abe's freedom was threatened. He and his family were forced to flee from Cuba, arriving in Miami Beach, Florida, in 1961. Abe was 36 years old and was forced to build a new life for himself and his family—again.

Survival was an old game for Abe. He held many types of jobs to keep his family fed, until one day he discovered his talents in real estate. By 1965, he owned many properties in Miami Beach, Florida, and once again rose to prominence in the community as a respected business leader and a dedicated community activist. In 1985, Abe Resnick was elected commissioner of Miami Beach, the first Cuban-Jewish Holocaust survivor to be so honored. He was reelected three times and served until 1993, when he chose to retire. Abe was appointed to the Executive Council of the Holocaust Museum in Washington, D.C., by President Bush in 1992, and is one of the founders of the Holocaust Memorial in Miami Beach.

Today, Abe is a man at peace with himself, living in Miami Beach with his wife, two sons, and six grandchildren—all of whom are very proud of their grandfather. As Abraham Resnickowitz, he survived the horrors of the Holocaust. As Abe Resnick, he built a life dedicated to serving others— a life based on a commitment to humanity. How proud his parents and sisters would be.

Reaching Beyond

1. The Kovno Ghetto is one of the most well-known of the ghettos established by the Nazis. Research this ghetto to learn what life was like for those imprisoned within its boundaries.

2. After escaping from the ghetto, Abe joined one of the partisan groups. Who were the partisans? What part did they play in the war effort against the Nazis?

3. What is your definition of a "survivor"? How does Abe meet this description?

4. What impressed you most about Abe and the way in which he has lived his life?

THROUGH THEIR EYES
A young girl hurled into hell

Dina Abelson, a librarian at Kimball School in Concord, New Hampshire, survived Auschwitz. Half a century later, she tells her story.

By RICHARD MERTENS
Concord Monitor, Concord, N.H.

In some ways her childhood was like any child's. She was born on July 10, 1929, the sixth child of Sara and Israel Lipschitz, a middle-class Jewish couple in the Polish city of Radom. As a girl she climbed apple trees and played make-believe. Once she fell in a river. She usually ate hunched over a book.

Then war came. She was 10 when the Germans invaded Poland, occupied Radom and closed the Jewish schools. Later they forced the family into a ghetto.

Those were years filled with fear and hunger, deportations and shootings. She still read books, some of them smuggled like chickens past ghetto guards. But a month after her 15th birthday, the remaining Jews of Radom were driven out. The SS marched them for three days in the August heat. At the end of the march they forced them into cattle cars.

Eight months later, the war was over. Almost miraculously, Dina Abelson lived, together with six of the other nine members of her family. Eventually they all came to the United States.

In recent years has she begun to talk about her past. Indeed, by the time they go on to Rundlett Junior High School, most of the students at Kimball School know the outlines of her experience.

"I'm growing older," she said recently. "I feel like most people who are survivors, that I have to tell it before it is too late."

Anyone who sees her in the Kimball School library will find it hard to imagine that this gentle, book-loving woman has lived through the most terrible episode of this violent century. She not only lived, she flourished. She raised a family and found work she loves. Her life has defied its violent beginning. Her service to learning, and to generations of schoolchildren, can never erase the scars. But it has enriched her life, and many others'.

In her own words

I was born in the suburbs of Radom. That's where the tannery was that my father owned. My father had a partner, but he was the tanning expert. That's how we survived the war. The Germans needed leather. So they kept us alive.

We were comfortable in comparison to others. We had a maid and someone to do the laundry, and for a while a nanny to take care of the children. Still it was rather primitive. The stove was still heated by wood.

I have fond memories of this time. We were very much together as a family. I realize now how much. We were secure. And as sixth in line, with four older brothers, I was spoiled. To this day my brothers think of me as a little girl. They worry if I can cross the street. They were very protective.

I liked school very much. I still like school. I'm a perennial student. I love it when I'm in a learning setting. It's the only time I really forget everything.

My father was a great reader. Books were like holy books. They were treated with great reverence. We had fairy tales, which were scary. I read *Anne of Green Gables*; I remember loving it and identifying with Anne. She also had red hair. But we didn't have the array of picture books they have now. So I read the grown-ups' books. I read *Nana* by Emile Zola. I read American writers in Polish. Hemingway was our favorite. Later on we read Schiller and Goethe. I don't remember having a meal without a book.

I don't know why I liked books. But now I know they saved my life.

I really believe that. If I didn't have books, my life would have been very much poorer. Particularly because I didn't have much formal education. I always preferred to read books that you really have to strain your brain to read.

The Polish people were not very kind to us. I was always a little frightened. Every night I said a prayer that I should survive the night and that no one should kill me in my bed. Particularly in the last few years before the war, you heard so much about pogroms in Russia—some closer. They used to throw rocks at us. We were very frightened.

I remember the war coming quite vividly. They closed all the schools—for Jewish people at least. Before that we had the bombing. We had to hide in the cellar.

The bombing was not very severe. It lasted just a week or so. The Germans came in right away and occupied the city. That's when the Polish people were cruel to us. They pointed a finger at us, because of course the Germans didn't know who was Jewish. My brothers ran toward the Russian border because they were taking all the men for the army or to kill them. They never made it that far. They were caught and brought back.

They took away our apartment first of all. We moved to a ghetto, then a smaller ghetto. Whenever we heard Germans come with dogs we hid. We held our breath and kept very quiet, so they wouldn't know we were there. They took away other children. If we didn't hide we would be taken away. We were too young to work.

My brother taught me Latin in the kitchen, sitting around a stove. We had to decline and conjugate. Whenever I see him now I say I have to be grateful to him. Languages came easy to me once I knew Latin.

I had a crush on my brother's best friend, so I wasn't a very good student. He was so handsome. I couldn't concentrate, gazing at him admiringly. He got killed.

People did smuggle in books. My brother's in-laws always had books. I remember reading at their place. I read *Gone with the Wind*—it was translated immediately into different languages. I really loved it.

Our main worry was to have a bed to sleep in and food to eat. At that time we were rather hungry. We didn't have too much. You were on your own to organize food. I guess we sold our belongings. My brothers still went to work outside the ghetto. They were able to trade, and they brought us food. I remember one brother tied a chicken to his legs and smuggled it in. It was starvation, but not of the magnitude later on. We ate a lot of soup. That's how we survived. Of course, my mother cooked for everybody.

We kept moving into smaller ghettos as they got rid of people. They would round people up and take all the children and older people. They killed a lot of us. They were shooting people every night. By the time we got to the little ghetto, there was just one street.

We worried all the time. We were afraid of being taken away and shot. They rounded up people, and you could hear shots from afar. I had nightmares about it for years afterward. There were not many places to hide. We were hiding later on in a furniture factory. The owner was a German who had taken over a Polish factory. My brother Al was a linguist and spoke perfect German. So he got a job at the factory. When there were selections to be held, he hid Bella, Myra, my mother and me. The men went to work.

I remember sitting with my mother and two sisters. I was so sleepy. You know sometimes you're so sleepy, but you can't sleep because you're not allowed to? I was sitting next to a piece of furniture, a table or something. My head kept hitting it. I wanted to sleep. It was one of those things you just can't forget. If we had not hid in the furniture factory, we wouldn't have survived the war.

In 1944, in August, we walked to the train. That was the first time I ever saw dead bodies. In the ghettos you heard the shots but didn't see the bodies. I remember seeing dead bodies lying there, almost stepping on them. If somebody stumbled, they didn't like that. If you couldn't get up, that was it. They just yelled and hit them with a gun in the back. If somebody couldn't get up, they just left them there.

It was a long march. It took three days. We slept in the fields. I was crying. It was very hot, very hot. I remember wanting a drink. I was so parched. I don't think we were given water. Maybe somebody gave me something—was it two cherries?

I think I tried to obliterate completely the experience. We didn't want to remember. I don't think I could go on living if I remembered the details of that march to the trains.

I remember being pushed into the car. They just rushed us. They told us, "'Rein! 'Rein!" I wanted to keep next to my brothers and sisters. I tried to keep close to help them. I thought I was grown up.

It was just a cattle train. There were no windows. There was nowhere to go to the bathroom. There was no air. The stench was terrible. I still remember, after all these years, the lack of air and the smell. Maybe that's why I'm so fussy now. I can't be in a room without fresh air. The rest I don't remember. I just blocked it out. I don't know how I survived it.

It wasn't very far to Auschwitz. But it seemed an eternity. We were half passed out for lack of air and food. And fear. Sometimes we just shut out of our minds the real world.

Then they opened the doors up. The train had stopped at the gate just for women—a women's camp. By then we were separated from my father and brothers. I didn't see them again until after the war.

They took us out. I don't remember anything until we were lined up and stripped. We had to undress completely. It was inside, and it was daytime. They took away pictures, jewelry—whatever we had

for possessions. There was a great commotion.

I was trying to stay close to my mother and my youngest sister. I was very annoyed that they separated us to cut my hair. The more beautiful hair they shaved off first. It took a lot of time. In the meantime they pulled my mother and Bella away. That was the last time I saw them.

That was the worst moment. We knew where they were going. We came in 1944; we already knew enough. The Germans maintained that we didn't know, but we knew.

Bella was the youngest. She was absolutely beautiful. She was like my baby. You know how an older child takes care of a younger child? I used to rock her to sleep. I carried her around. I was a very responsible, serious child.

I told myself at the end of the war, "If I had only stayed with my mother and Bella I could have saved them." Which is ridiculous, because I couldn't save them. Who was I, God? But it was very bad for me.

Mira and I made it by the skin of our teeth. We made ourselves older in order not to be killed. When they asked your age, you added a few years. They took away the children. My sister Bella was as big as I, taller even. But she told her age.

Surviving on dreams

I don't remember when they gave us our numbers. But I remember it hurting. You had to stand still.

We stayed in a wooden building. You've probably seen them in the movies, or in documentaries. I don't watch them. They were wooden huts. They were big, because there were many of us in one building.

The bathroom conditions were just horrible. Thousands of people used the same latrine at the same time. It was just a big trench.

We slept next to each other, eight across. The bunk was just planks with straw and this rough, gray, wool blanket. It was very difficult to sleep. But we must have slept. You just dozed off. I always dreamt I had a pillow.

The surprising thing is that I remember what I was thinking

about. Besides being hungry—that's such an overpowering sensation—I dreamt of what I would wear after the war. I dreamt about my favorite outfit, my navy blue pleated skirt, my white blouse and patent-leather shoes. That was how I was going to get dressed up.

We had women guards—German and Polish. They were big women. Or maybe it seemed that way because I was small. I remember one stepping on my sister. They threw her down. I don't know why.

We were very, very upset because we were separated from our families. We had people to talk to, although we weren't allowed to talk. I'm not sure what we did with our time. We tried not to get sick. They didn't allow sickness. They just did away with sick people. The doctors looked us over so often that we had to think about staying clean.

The selections were inside. I remember lights shining at us, inspecting us. It must have been done pretty often. Whoever didn't look good to them, went. They took you if you stood out, or if they didn't like your mannerisms. It was implied where you were going. It was almost self-evident by those who were selected.

We didn't work. We didn't do anything. I think we were thinking how hungry we were. We were in a perpetual state of gnawing hunger. We were given one bread for the week, the three of us. That's all. People stole the food, so we slept on it. They still stole it.

It was a small bread, and it was all moldy. We wondered whether we could get the bread before it was green, when there was still a little white in it. On Sunday we got soup made of potato peelings and grass or something. The soup was special. We got it if we behaved. It tasted all right. And on Sunday we got dessert: a piece not of peeling but of raw potato. Have you ever tried raw potato? I tried it after the war. It was terrible.

Hunger is such an overpowering thing. We didn't talk about anything else. Everyone dreamt about food. Just to have a loaf of bread to

yourself! That's all we thought about.

But we didn't eat just stale, hard moldy bread. We ate it with our imaginations. We tasted chocolate in it, bananas, oranges, pineapples—all the fruits that were rare in Poland at the time. It wasn't just me. My sister told me that she did, too.

I guess that's how we survived. If we had just tasted moldy bread, I don't think we could have swallowed. But it was just barely enough to survive. The things we ate didn't have any vitamins at all, particularly Vitamin C. After the war I had great problems with my teeth because of scurvy.

I remember my brother's sister-in-law singing for soup. Her name was Paula. She had a beautiful voice, and the women who watched us found out. If she sang for them, they gave her all the soup she wanted. She used to give me and my sisters some in a little tin cup.

The unmentionable

I remember the torture. We were awakened at 4 or 5 for the morning call—the Appell. If someone was missing we had to kneel on stones until they found the person. Very few people tried to get away. They might just have forgotten to come. I still remember the feel of the stones going into my knees, and waiting, hoping the person would show up. We would kneel for hours.

Of course there was barbed wire. We were surrounded by it. It was an electrified fence. And we could also see the unmentionable from afar—the gas chambers. We didn't see the buildings, but we saw the skyline—and the smoke. But I didn't let myself know. I think I just shut it out completely. The fact is, we knew the fate of my mother and sister. I often have a picture in my mind of them entering the gas chambers.

If it's too painful, you try to bury it. It's not completely possible. It comes out in one way or another. I had nightmares for many years.

I remember being outside, watching other people arriving. We

were rather hardy because we knew suffering already. We had gone gradually through all the ghettos and the persecutions of the Polish people even before the war. We had been slowly conditioned for hardship.

The new arrivals were from Italy, girls in high heels and silk dresses. They hadn't gone through a ghetto as we had. They had just been taken off the streets, right from normal life. They were beautiful girls from well-to-do families. They became our friends because of Paula. They sang too. They sang arias from operas. We admired them. In some ways, we were jealous. But they died, because they were not used to the life. They just didn't know anything about it. They were like little flowers taken off their stems.

Despite everything, no one committed suicide. It would have been easy. All you had to do was touch the barbed wire. Only one person tried to run away. I didn't know if she didn't succeed or if she died or what. We stood for hours and hours that time. I guess we still hoped. You never give up as long as you have hope. I guess we hoped that any day it would be over.

We didn't stay until winter. We went to Ravensbruck. I don't recall how we got there. Probably in trucks. It was a big station, where they separated us. We were divided into groups to send to work or not to work—or death.

We went to Malchow. It was a work camp. We lived in a barracks, and we marched to a place underground every day. We did it at night. It was winter, and we marched in wooden shoes. I remember my feet were so cold. It's not so easy to walk in wooden shoes. My shoes kept falling off. Part of a foot was bandaged. But we had to keep in step, and we had to keep awake. You couldn't fall behind. If one has to do something, sometimes one finds the strength. It did happen once, when I was walking in those shoes that a soldier helped me up. He was one of the guards. He knew that he needed to protect me from the other guards.

Somebody would have put a gun to my head or something. He helped me up and then he gave me some water from his canteen.

I wonder how I could take what we did and function normally? Of course we were rather resilient at that age. The younger the person was, the easier it was. The old people were gone by that time.

My older sister, Rose, got so emaciated. She was very beautiful. She was as pretty as Dorothy Lamour. All of a sudden she looked like a bag of bones. She was 18.

I was very young. To this day I feel very young. I was never really a teenager. I went right from childhood to adulthood.

Put to work
We worked at an arms plant. It was camouflaged, with trees on top. The place was dangerous because of Allied bombing. It was very hard to work at night. We had to weigh gunpowder, just the right amount. I have a picture in my mind sitting with a little scale—like a toy scale. You had to measure the same amount every time.

It was mesmerizing. It made you sleepy. I kept myself awake so I wouldn't be hit. No wonder I'm an insomniac now, when you think of it. If someone wakes me up, they apologize. They know sleep comes dear to me.

We had to be so careful. But we must have been able to do it, because they didn't kill us. I don't know what they used the gunpowder for. I'm sure they used it. To think that I measured powder for them to shoot us!

We slept a lot during the day. At that point we were just like little vegetables. But we hoped that it would be over, that better times were coming. We got news that it wouldn't be long. The front was very close. We heard the airplanes. I remember hearing people talking, "The Americans are coming!"

I don't know how we survived. I guess it shows how strong human beings are. We didn't want to die. I think we lived with hope. I fell into pieces when it was over and I realized what I had gone through.

Liberated, but not free from the memories
We were liberated just a few days before the end of the war. But you never know. They might have killed us when they were backing up. They did that in many places. They killed people when they knew the Allies were near.

The Swedish Red Cross exchanged us for German prisoners in Norway. They swapped us one for one. They took everybody from that particular camp.

We traveled in open trucks with white crosses on them. Once I saw the crosses, I knew I was free. That's when I started missing my mother and sister. I didn't know about the men. But I was starting to feel sad.

We went to a train station in Denmark. I don't remember much about the trip. The Allied bombs were falling around us. A girl lost one of her arms. The Red Cross gave us coffee and donuts. Everywhere, they gave out donuts. I didn't know what a donut was. I took one bite of it and got sick. To this day I can't eat a donut.

Soon we found ourselves in a beautiful train, first class, with silver settings and waiters in white gloves. I remember someone came over with something really delicious to eat. But I couldn't eat. I couldn't touch the food. Can you imagine? After all that hunger!

On the way to Sweden I realized my loss. I cried and cried. I cried my soul out. I remember many times thinking that my mother and sister should be here. I wanted to be dead. I thought, "Why am I alive?" I almost resented that I was a survivor. Why did I survive? To be in pain now? Which is really quite unrealistic. But it bothered me for a long time that I was alive and they were not.

Before, I guess, I had hoped. But going to Sweden, I was hysterical. I did not feel joy at being liberated. The saddest thing was being liberated and not being able to help the rest of your family. I'll never get over my mother's death. I can't even use the word. My mother-in-law once asked me why I don't call her "Mother." I explained, and she never asked me again.

I was completely devastated. But one has to go on. The Swedish people were so kind to us. I really have a soft spot for them. Even today, when I see a Swedish child, it does something to me.

At first we were in Malmo at a school turned into a hospital. We were in bed most of the time. I'm small. Even now I don't weigh that much. But I was just a bag of bones.

I remember people in white bending over me. They knew what they were doing. At first they fed us intravenously. They also fed us farina—cream of wheat. Everything we ate was ground up like baby food. After the war a lot of people died from eating regular food.

We didn't stay in one place for long. We were constantly moved. Finally we settled at one place, near Stockholm. We worked there half a day making brushes. The other half was schooling.

Finding each other
The whole school was going to go to Israel, except for a few with families in Argentina. We were signed up and everything. We had to go somewhere, I guess. I didn't know where else to go.

At the last minute we decided to go to Germany to see what the rest of the family was doing. My brother Al was going to America. He wanted us to go there, not to Israel. He told us how wonderful it was in America. It was a good thing, because the others landed in Cyprus and the boat was attacked. The British imprisoned them on Cyprus.

Arriving in America
I don't remember arriving in New York. Everyone talks about seeing Miss Liberty, but I remember staring out at the ocean, not that. Maybe my mind was occupied with something else. Or maybe I was sad.

Reprinted with permission from *Concord Monitor* and Dina Abelson.

Reaching Beyond

1. Why is it so important that Dina Abelson and other Holocaust survivors share their experiences with today's youth?

2. How do the experiences described by Dina Abelson mirror the events of and leading to the Holocaust as described in this chapter?

3. How does Dina Abelson's story add to your understanding of the Holocaust? Did this testimony change your attitudes and/or understanding of the Holocaust? If so, explain.

4. What message do you think Dina Abelson would especially like to impart to students your age?

THROUGH THEIR EYES

ANA'S STORY

The following are portions of an eyewitness account—one person's remembrances of the Holocaust.

"My name is Ana Jinno. I was born in Kosicé, a city in the Eastern part of Czechoslovakia on December 1, 1936...

[In 1938] my parents and I moved to Liptovsky Svety Mikulash, a town in the lower Tatra, which is located in the middle of Slovakia. There my father was employed as an engineer at a very important building company. Shortly after we moved from Kosicé, in the year 1939, that eastern part of Slovakia was attached to Hungary, so we got cut off from my mother's family. This happened at the time when Czechoslovakia capitulated to the Germans and was divided into two countries. The Czech part was occupied by the Nazis and in Slovakia a fashistik [fascist], collaborationist government was formed.

I wish to make clear that all this story is based on my memories, as I remember them from my childhood, with a child's outlook, and that I am not consulting any documents.

I remember the fear, the clear knowledge that we could be taken to the camps at any time or simply shot, only for being Jews. I remember Nazis coming one evening into our small apartment, and taking away all valuable things we had. I remember my parents bringing home with joy our first radio, and having it taken away by the Nazis the next day. I remember long, long evenings in winter sitting at home because Jews were not permitted to walk on the streets after dusk. And of course, I remember the yellow Magen David, which is now the proud symbol of our nation [Israel], but at that time was a symbol of humiliation and of the threatening death sentence floating above all Jews...

I started going to school, so I suppose the year was 1942–43. Naturally, we were only allowed to go to Jewish schools, and there was only one Jewish teacher, an elderly gentleman... After a few months, one day I came to school in the morning, and the gates were closed. The teacher had been taken away to an extermination camp...

One gloomy night, some Slovakian gendarmes, which were the policemen of the Slovakian collaborationist government, came rudely into our home and took my father away to the concentration camp in Zhilina, Slovakia, where they temporarily kept the Jews they had seized before transferring them to the extermination camps... So now my mother and I were alone in the midst of this horror... Nevertheless, my mother never gave up. She immediately contacted my father's employer, who was a Czech engineer, and he in turn got in touch with some influential people he knew, in order to have my father released. My father was his right hand, and it was very important for this man to have my father released. At that time it was still possible...

A few weeks passed, and after many ordeals, my dear father was released and came back to us. He looked like the shadow of himself, but he was back with us. I vaguely recall some of the stories he told us about the concentration camp in Zhilina—how the Nazis and the Slovakian collaborationist police came into their barracks, precisely when the religious Jews were saying their prayers, and hit them brutally and also how they kicked them around and tore out the hairs of their beards, one by one, while laughing their cruel laughter...

The year, I suppose, was 1944. When my parents heard about my grandparents, aunt and uncle being closed up in a ghetto, from where they probably would be deported, they panicked. My mother was desperate. Fortunately, my father was still in a position to pull some strings, through his employer, and had them brought over, illegally of course. At the same time, the situation was already getting bad for us too...

This was the time when the partisan uprising began in the woods of Slovakia. My father decided to join the fighters, but before that, he had to find a safe hiding place for the rest of us. He also provided himself and us with false documents, under the surname of Kalina, a gentile, Slavic name. Naturally, we were to appear as non-Jews, more precisely as Protestants. This was the religion that appeared on the documents. So he started looking for a hiding place. There are many caves in that part of the Slovakian woods, and that was what he was looking for. A good, safe cave, for his family to spend the winter, while he would be fighting against the Nazis.

He knew some peasants from the surrounding villages. He was acquainted with them through his work in building roads. They were very good people and they helped us a lot. It was also agreed that they would provide us with food. I must remind you all that they were doing this at the risk of their own lives.

This was already late summer, 1944. I was almost eight years old. I remember the long walks we took in the woods, searching for an appropriate place to hide. To me, a child, they were like outings, although the fear was there, and the anxiety, and I knew exactly what was going on and that terrible things might happen to us. I can even remember the smell of the musk and of the pine trees. The odors of my childhood!

Finally, after a few weeks' searching, we found an appropriate cave, which might be "comfortable," ironically speaking for a whole family to spend as much time as was necessary, till the horror was over...

Then my mother discovered that she was pregnant. In spite of that, she decided that she would take me and "accompany" my father to where he had to join the Partisans, and then come back. Don't ask me how she planned to do it, as all that region was filled with Nazis, but she was very attached to my father and perhaps she wanted to postpone the parting, or maybe she never thought of coming back without him but to go wherever he went, for better or for worse... It was early autumn, the sun was warm and pleasant. Wild berries were all scattered on the green grass carpet. And then when my mother wanted to return to where her family was staying in a cave, it turned out to be impossible. So here was a pregnant woman and a seven-year-old girl, part of a Partisan group.

We walked and walked, and when the men went to fight, we stayed hidden in the woods. Till now we were lucky, we hadn't been caught. There was no food, and we were hungry... And then it started raining and pouring, and walking became more difficult because of the mud... In the morning the autumn sun was shining brightly, and after stretching out our painful limbs, we continued on our way. Suddenly we saw a house and a wooden hut by it. Some of the men went carefully to find out who was living there. It turned out to be the wood keeper's house, and he was willing to let us stay in the wooden hut. We were a group of about twenty...

My mother got a "job" with the wood keeper's wife, to cook and clean for her, and in return she got some food. I had a treat that day; my mother cooked some jam. I was with her in the kitchen, and I got a piece of bread with strawberry jam. It tasted good. A day or two after that, while playing in the sun outside the hut, I heard a very loud noise. I ran inside in panic and when some of the grown-ups looked out, they saw that we were surrounded by German tanks. Had the wood keeper turned us in? Maybe.

They started shooting at us with their submachine guns and there was no other choice but to turn ourselves in... The German headquarters were in a nearby village, in the priest's house. It wasn't the priest's fault, they simply occupied his house...

Here I want to explain something to you: In Czechoslovakia most if not all Jews knew German and so did my parents. On the other hand, gentile Slovaks, and especially villagers (which we were supposed to be), didn't know German. So my parents had to pretend they didn't understand anything that was said by the soldiers.

Once we were inside, my mother asked for an interpreter... she asked to be heard by an officer... We entered a big room and she couldn't believe her eyes. A whole panel of officers were waiting to hear her story. Of course she spoke in Slovakian and with an interpreter. She was trembling with fear but she knew that she had to go through this, that it was a matter of life or death. And this was her story: First she asked how they suspect her, a pregnant woman with a child, of being a Partisan. In response, the Germans asked her if we weren't such, how come we were wandering about the woods with a Partisan group. And then she made up the most incredible story. She said that we were visiting her parents at a nearby village and we wanted to return to our place of residence, the city of Nitra (our false documents stated that city as our place of residence) in the west of Slovakia, near the capital Bratislava, but as she had been told that the Germans killed the unborn babies of pregnant women, she was so terribly frightened that she felt more protected to walk with a group of armed men through the woods. But no, not to fight, never... she wouldn't let her husband do such a thing. And then she burst into tears...

The officers belonged to the Wermacht, which was the regular German Army and were much less sophisticated in their cruelty than the Gestapo. After hearing my mother's words, they started to laugh. They laughed and laughed and couldn't stop. Afterwards they told us to leave the room...

With dawn, the Czech-speaking soldier knocked on the door, and told us to get dressed and that we were released. Naturally, my mother wouldn't leave without my father, but the soldier assured her that he was waiting for us outside and that he had been released too... Later on we found out that all the rest of the group had been executed...

I can't recall now how finally we got to Nitra, but we did. There my parents looked for a furnished room. I don't know what kind of story they told the landlords, because this was not a region friendly to Partisans and refugees, or people who were suspected of being run-away Jews. So I am sure that my parents must have made up some very convincing story...

In April the bombardments started in our region... I'm not going to describe the horrors of a city being bombarded, as all of us have seen it many, many times in pictures and most of all because I don't feel up to it. I don't feel up to describing what I saw then through a child's eyes.

Towards the end of April 1945, the city of Nitra was liberated. The Russian soldiers marched in. During the night of the 28th or 29th, my mother was taken to a hospital through the burning city and she gave birth to a beautiful baby girl. We gave her a Russian name, Katerina, and now we call her Kathy.

How we got back to my birth town, Kosicé, in the east of Slovakia, which had been Hungary during the war, as you may well remember, and now was again part of Czechoslovakia, is a long story which I want to make short. We got on a cart driven by horses (or maybe it was oxen?) with a tiny baby in our arms, and this way we crossed Slovakia. We gave golden coins for a piece of bread... When we arrived in Kosicé, my mother's parents, brothers and sister were happily back from the cave in which they had spent a cruel winter. All safe and sound. On the other hand my father's family was all gone and buried...

And what next? Life goes on. In 1948, just before the communist regime took over in Czechoslovakia, we emigrated to Uruguay. We found a warm, hospitable, unprejudiced people, both Jews and Gentiles. There I went to school, got married, and gave birth to two girls and one boy, and there, regretfully, I buried my 56-year-old father.

In 1970, my husband and I decided that we wanted to bring up our children in Israel...About eight years later, my sister and her family joined us, and a year after that my mother did so too.

Our children are strong, free, proud sabras. The older daughter, Gabby, is a travel agent, our son Erez is a composer and our younger daughter, Galit, is a member of a kibbutz. She is married and in a few months time I will be a happy grandmother.

Tell me, don't you believe in miracles?

Reaching Beyond

1. Where are Hungary and Czechoslovakia located? What countries border them?

2. Who were the Partisans? What part did they play in fighting the Nazis?

3. What people, other than family, helped Ana survive? What part did they play?

4. How did Ana's mother save her family from certain death?

5. Why does Ana consider herself to be so fortunate? Does this attitude seem to be common among survivors? Explain.

The forest was a refuge from death, a place to hide. The forest was also a vast cemetery where many victims met their death. It was a forest such as this that hid Abe and Ana.

ALL THROUGH THE NIGHT:
THE HOLOCAUST YEARS—1933-1945

REFLECTIONS

1. Beginning with Kristallnacht, what systematic steps did the Nazis take that led to the Holocaust?

2. Why were the Nazis so successful in their attempts to exterminate the Jewish people?

3. What responsibility do the United States and other countries have to protect groups of people from mass annihilation? Did the United States live up to this responsibility during the Holocaust years? Explain.

4. Why are so many people afraid to take a stand and get involved when they see an injustice? What can each of us do to change this?

5. In a civilized society, what qualities give people their "humanity"? Did the Nazis exhibit these qualities? Explain.

6. Think of all the lessons of the Holocaust. What one lesson of the Holocaust is the most important to you? Have a class discussion on the lessons of the Holocaust as each student discusses his/her responses.

EXTENSIONS

1. Study the Nuremberg Laws on pages 12 and 13. Which part(s) of the Nuremberg Laws do you find most disturbing? Explain.

2. To gain an understanding of the chronology of events of the Holocaust, create a class time line. Each group of students can select a different year, from 1933–1945, and list the significant events of the year as they concern the Holocaust. As a class, develop a creative design for the time line.

3. Read another book that describes the Holocaust (see Resources), such as *The War Against the Jews 1933–1945* by Lucy Dawidowicz (Bantam, 1986) or Milton Meltzer's *Never to Forget: The Jews of the Holocaust* (Dell, 1977). Select three pieces of information that you found new and especially relevant. Write each on a separate index card and share the information with the class. Create a class Holocaust card file with these cards for future reference.

4. Imagine that you were in the position to rescue another human being but at a risk to your own life or the lives of those in your family. Make a list of reasons to support a decision to become a rescuer and make another list that includes the reasons why you should not be a rescuer. Have a class discussion based on this issue, using your list to help you focus on some of the main points involved.

5. There are many agencies to which you can write requesting information on the Holocaust (see Resources). Send away for this information and create a Holocaust information center in your classroom.

6. Write an essay to express your feelings about any aspect of the Holocaust. You may wish to base your essay on the historical notes or stories from this chapter. You may wish to base your essay on any of the photographs of the Holocaust or you may wish to explore an idea that especially affected you in your reading of the literature of the Holocaust.

CHAPTER 3

A New Dawn: Liberation, Rebirth, and the Nuremberg Trials

"For the dead and the living we must bear witness."

Elie Wiesel

HISTORICAL NOTES

A NEW DAWN:
LIBERATION, REBIRTH, AND THE NUREMBERG TRIALS

Liberation—April 1945–June 1945

In the final days of World War II, there were more than 700,000 prisoners still in concentration camps throughout Eastern Europe. As the Russian Army began its final advances from the east and as the Allied forces approached from the west, the Nazi soldiers, with insufficient time to kill those who remained, began moving the prisoners out, trying to keep ahead of the advancing armies. Men, women, and children were once again forced into cattle cars, transported to more distant camps; others were marched along hundreds of miles in the freezing cold. Many prisoners, already suffering from a multitude of diseases and nearly dead from a combination of starvation, exhaustion, and overexposure to the harsh elements, could not survive these final efforts to destroy them. In the last days of the war, approximately half of the remaining prisoners died.

Into this gray world of death and despair marched the liberators, shining stars among the ashes of darkness. Even in the last moments, as the liberators entered the camps, they reported hearing shots—the guards were shooting the last survivors. Eye-witness testimonies of what they saw have been given by a great number of liberators, including former President Dwight David Eisenhower, then a general of the U.S. forces. In a letter to General George C. Marshall, Eisenhower gives this account of Ohrdruf concentration camp:

> The things I saw beggar description...The visual evidence and
> the verbal testimony of starvation, cruelty, and bestiality were so
> overpowering as to leave me a bit sick...I made the visit deliberately,
> in order to be in a position to give first-hand evidence of these things if
> ever, in the future, there develops a tendency to charge these allegations
> merely to propaganda.
>
> April 15, 1945

Eisenhower was not alone in his shock and revulsion over what he saw—the suffering humans are capable of inflicting, the suffering humans had to endure.

One liberator, Dr. Leon Bass, a former teacher and principal from Philadelphia, often tours the country, spending much of his time giving talks to students to make them aware of the atrocities of the Holocaust. Bass was part of the 183rd Unit which liberated Buchenwald. He was only 19 years old but the images he witnessed have made an indelible imprint upon him. Bass did not speak of these horrors for over 20 years, not until 1968, when a survivor of the Holocaust addressed the students in his school and was virtually ignored. Bass knew he could no longer remain silent. He knew that the history of the Holocaust had to be told, had to be remembered, had to be given a voice. (Dr. Bass' eye-witness account is included on pages 44–45.)

As World War II came to an end and the camps were liberated, other survivors began to emerge from their hiding places. Some had been hidden by Christians in cellars and attics. Some had hidden in caves and in forests and in holes in the ground. And now, their only wish was to return home. But, they no longer had a home—Jewish homes had been confiscated and their possessions taken—nor did they have a country to which they could return. A few, who tried to return to their homes in Poland, were greeted with widespread anti-Semitism. In fact, in the summer of 1946, thousands of Jews were killed in a mass pogrom in Poland. Sadly, hatred and racism still existed less than one year after the Holocaust.

Liberation brought to a close the most tragic chapter in the history of humankind. A tragedy so overwhelming, so brutal, so horrific, that to this day it boggles the imagination. And, as this chapter closed, another one began...a chapter filled with the pain of searching for friends and family who no longer existed; a chapter filled with the determination and courage needed to start life over again; a chapter that gives testimony to the triumph of the human spirit.

Rebirth

Survivors, with no place to go, no country, no home, no family, were now "Displaced Persons." Displaced Persons Camps (DP Camps) were set up in Germany, Austria, and Italy. By 1947, there were approximately 250,000 Jews in these camps, the largest of which was Bergen-Belsen. Survivors had such a strong will to live that they developed an obsession to bring normalcy to their world. Few children survived the Holocaust, but within one year, 2,000 babies were born in Bergen-Belsen alone. These children, and others born out of the flames of the Holocaust, are now known as "children of survivors of the Holocaust." Cultural activities quickly flourished in the DP Camps, and the first Jewish newspaper, handwritten, appeared only weeks after liberation.

The main hope of the survivors was to leave their camps and resettle outside Europe and begin new lives. But just because the war was over, it did not mean that the world would welcome the Jewish people with open arms. Little changed regarding immigration policy, and for thousands and thousands of Jewish survivors, the DP camps would be their only homes for two to three years.

Eventually, over the course of many years, almost two-thirds of the survivors of the Holocaust settled in Israel. But the struggle to emigrate there and to establish a Jewish Homeland was a long and dangerous one.

Bericha is a Hebrew word meaning "flight." It refers to flight from the past—flight to a new beginning in Israel. Fleeing the past, however, has always been difficult for the Jewish people, and the end of World War II brought little relief. Immigration to the United States, as mentioned earlier, was still very limited, and immigration to Israel, limited in 1939 by a British mandate known as the White Paper, was equally difficult. Despite the horrible circumstances of the Jews of Eastern Europe, Britain had done little to amend immigration policy. At the end of World War II, those Jewish people who did reach Israel (then Palestine) illegally were placed in detention camps in Cyprus. British soldiers were sent to Israel to help keep survivors of the Holocaust from entering the country. As a result, the Hebrew Movement of Revolt, an underground organization which was part of the Haganah (the underground Jewish defense forces) was formed to fight the British. Never again would the Jewish people be defenseless. Never again would they allow the atrocities of the Holocaust to happen to them. They were ready to fight. For years, this group smuggled groups onto the shores of Israel. Despite British attempts to stop them, between 1944 and 1947 almost 100,000 survivors from Europe managed to reach Israel in 64 ships. Today the children and grandchildren of the Holocaust survivors who made "Bericha" can be seen walking proudly on the streets of their new homeland, Israel, which in 1949 became an independent nation, free of British control.

Today the survivors of the Holocaust live in all parts of the world. These men and women have made incredible contributions in all areas of endeavor. Their success, in large measure, was due to, as William B. Helmreich explains in his book *Against All Odds: Holocaust Survivors and the Successful Lives They Made in America,* "... hard work and determination, skill and intelligence, luck, and a willingness to take risks." The survivors of the Holocaust raised a generation of sons and daughters who respect life and who strive to make their own contributions to our world.

The Nuremberg Trials

In 1941 and 1942, when reports and information were being relayed to the Allied powers about the atrocities taking place in Eastern Europe, the leaders of the major allied countries, the United States, France, Russia, and England, warned Germany that there would be retribution. President Roosevelt publicly proclaimed that the Nazis would be punished. When the war was over, these promises were kept.

Each year thousands of trees are planted in Israel in memory of the 6,000,000 who died in the Holocaust and as a symbol of renewal and rebirth.

The International Military Tribunal convened in 1945, in Nuremberg, Germany. The Nuremberg Trials, as they are now called, tried 22 leaders of the Nazi Regime for their unconscionable acts of murder and genocide during World War II. These leaders included Hermann Göring, chief of the air force and second in command to Adolf Hitler; Rudolf Höss, the Reich Minister, ranked third in seniority; and Ernst Kaltrenbrunner, head of the Security Police. (It is believed that Adolf Hitler committed suicide in April 1945.) The trials were organized by the United States, the Soviet Union, Great Britain, and France. The Nazi leaders were charged with crimes against peace, war crimes, and crimes against humanity. Nineteen of the 22 defendants were found guilty. Of these, 12 were sentenced to death by hanging, 3 to life imprisonment, and 4 to prison terms of between 10 to 20 years.

The Nuremberg Trials were important for a number of critical reasons. Photographs and other evidence of the Holocaust were gathered and presented at the Nuremberg Trials. This evidence has helped to provide us with the tremendous amount of documentation of the Holocaust that is in existence today, including many secret Nazi letters and memos. Perhaps the most significant result of the trials was that a moral decision was made which has had far-reaching implications. This decision rejected the argument that people who are "just following orders" have no responsibility for the orders they carry out. The trials emphasized the idea that each of us—soldier and civilian alike—has a moral obligation to disobey orders which are inhuman, orders which are fundamentally wrong. Since the Nuremberg Trials, other Nazi leaders have been brought to trial. These trials are about justice, not revenge. One of the most famous of these was the trial of Adolf Eichmann, held in Jerusalem. This trial opened the eyes of the world to the atrocities of the Holocaust, for it was here that many survivors gave testimonies. Unfortunately, not all Nazi war criminals have been brought to trial. Many more Nazi leaders went into hiding in countries around the world, including the United States.

The Office of Special Investigations (O.S. I.), a U.S. governmental agency, is still in constant search of Nazi war criminals, as are other private groups. Society cannot condone evil and each individual must be held accountable for his/her actions. Acts of brutality, acts that deny others their fundamental rights, must not go unpunished. We must all keep a constant vigil against prejudice, discrimination, and hate.

THROUGH THEIR EYES

TESTIMONY OF A LIBERATOR—
DR. LEON BASS

Dr. Bass is an African-American soldier who helped liberate Buchenwald Concentration Camp at the end of World War II. The following are excerpts from a talk Dr. Bass gave to students at English High School in Boston.

...The war appeared to be over, and our unit went to a place called Weimar. Weimar today is in East Germany, but at that time there was no East Germany—just Germany...Immediately about five or six of us took off with one of our officers to a place called Buchenwald...Buchenwald was a concentration camp. I had no idea of what kind of camp this was. I thought it might have been a prisoner-of-war camp where they kept soldiers who were captured. But on this day in 1945 I was to discover what human suffering was all about. I was going to take off the blinders that caused me to have tunnel vision. I was going to see clearly that, yes, I suffered and I was hurting because I was black in a white society, but I had also begun to understand that suffering is universal. It is not just relegated to me and mine; it touches us all. And so I walked through the gates of Buchenwald, and I saw the dead and the dying. I saw people who had been so brutalized and were so maltreated. They had been starved and beaten. They had been worked almost to death, not fed enough, no medical care. One man came up and his fingers were webbed together, all of his fingers together, by sores and scabs. This was due to malnutrition, not eating the proper foods. There were others holding on to each other, trying to remain standing. They had on wooden shoes; they had on the pajama-type uniform; their heads had been shaved. Some had the tattoos with numbers on their arms. I saw this. I saw them with the wooden bowls. Some of them were standing waiting for food and hitting on the fence (this was wire fence) and making guttural sounds—not words,—just sounds.

I said, "My God, what is this insanity that I have come to? What are these people here for? What have they done? What was their crime that would cause people to treat them like this?" You see, I wasn't prepared for this. I was only nineteen; I had no frame of reference to cope with the kind of thing I was witnessing....

I didn't come up to Boston just to tell you the horror story; as horrible as it is, the story must be told. History cannot be swept under the rug. It shouldn't be and you must not permit it to be. We have things in our history that are ugly; slavery was ugly...It was an evil, horrible institution and the Holocaust is just as evil, if not more so. There was a planned, organized, systematic approach to annihilating a whole group of people. They killed not only six million Jews but millions of others. There were Gypsies there, there were Catholics there, there were communists, trade unionists, homosexuals; anyone who didn't fit the scheme of things for the Nazis was in Buchenwald and all the other camps to be annihilated. They came pretty close to doing it too. But somebody had to stand up, somebody had to dare to be a Daniel and walk into the den and say, "This evil cannot continue..."

Reprinted with permission from Dr. Leon Bass

Reaching Beyond

1. What do you think Dr. Bass thought he would find when he liberated Buchenwald? How did his expectations differ from reality?

2. Dr. Bass said, "...I was going to take off the blinders that caused me to have tunnel vision. I was going to see clearly that, yes, I suffered and I was hurting because I was black in a white society, but I had also begun to understand that suffering is universal..." What did he mean when he said he had had tunnel vision? What important lessons did Dr. Bass discover about suffering after his experiences at Buchenwald?

3. Why does Dr. Bass tour the country, making students aware of the Holocaust?

4. What do you believe is the most important message the students at English High gained from hearing Dr. Bass talk?

A NEW DAWN:
LIBERATION, REBIRTH, AND
THE NUREMBERG TRIALS

REFLECTIONS

1. Why did former president Dwight D. Eisenhower believe it imperative that he give testimony concerning what he saw when he and his troops liberated some of the concentration camps?

2. What did the liberators witness when they entered the concentration camps? Why was it impossible for any of the liberators to be prepared for what they witnessed in the concentration camps? Explain.

3. What hardships did the survivors of the Holocaust have to overcome as they tried to put the pieces of their lives back together?

4. Liberation freed the victims physically, but not emotionally. Explain this contradiction.

5. Discuss the importance of the Nuremberg Trials. Of all the outcomes, which do you believe is most significant? Explain your answer.

EXTENSIONS

1. Read about the contributions made to this world by survivors of the Holocaust. With classmates, compile a list of these people and their accomplishments.

2. Read portions of the book *Against All Odds: Holocaust Survivors and the Successful Lives They Make in America* by William B. Helmreich (Simon and Schuster, 1993). Based on this book or other research you have done on this subject, explore the question "How do people who have gone through such adversity pick up the pieces of their lives?"

3. What lessons have the survivors of the Holocaust taught you? What lessons can we learn from them? Compile your responses into a booklet as a tribute to the survivors and to all those who have faced adversity and had to start life, in one way or another, over again.

4. Learn more about the Nuremberg Trials and other trials in which Nazi war criminals were forced to face up to their part in the Holocaust. Find out which Nazis were tried, what they were charged with, and the resulting sentences.

5. Several movies have been made which deal with the capture and trials of Nazi leaders. View one and discuss the way in which the movie dealt with the issue of justice. These movies include *Judgment at Nuremberg,* which tells the story of the Nuremberg Trials, and *The House on Garibaldi Street,* a fictionalized account of the trial of Nazi leader Adolf Eichmann.

CHAPTER 4

Resistance and Rescue: The Heroes and Heroines of the Holocaust

"Whoever saves a single soul, it is as if he saved the whole world."

The Talmud

4
HISTORICAL NOTES

RESISTANCE AND RESCUE:
THE HEROES AND HEROINES OF THE HOLOCAUST

If the Holocaust has taught us anything, it is that one person can make a difference. Thousands of lives were saved through the courage of those who not only refused to be a part of it, but who took action against hatred and tyranny. And while the numbers saved seem small in comparison to the 6,000,000 victims of the Holocaust, these heroes and heroines give us a legacy of hope and the belief that good can triumph over evil.

While the Holocaust gave rise to all types of heroes and heroines, from the mother who shielded her children from the Nazi bullets with her own body, to the prisoners in the concentration camps who gave away their own morsels of food to those dying of starvation, this chapter will focus on those heroes and heroines involved in resistance and rescue.

By resistance, we refer to those who defied the Nazis in some way. Resistance fighters smuggled foods, arms, and other necessities. Resistance fighters sabotaged the German munitions plants. Resistance fighters did battle in the mountains, in the forests, and behind the ghetto walls. Resistance fighters fought oppression and moral degradation. Resistance fighters did what they could, used what they had, to save a life, lift a soul, or stop the Nazis, if only for a moment in time.

The rescuers of the Holocaust are generally those individuals who risked their own lives to save another. Most of these rescuers were the men, women, and children of Europe who hid their neighbors in attics, in haystacks, and in secret closets. They are the farmers, the teachers, the wealthy, the poor, who offered food, shelter, and compassion. While most of these rescuers have lived in relative anonymity, several names, such as Raoul Wallenberg and Oskar Schindler, have become known throughout the world.

In addition to the individual courage exhibited, small villages, organized groups, and even nations banded together to resist the Nazi cruelty. The people of Le Chambon, a village in south central France, publicly refused to aid the Nazi effort; a student group in Holland devoted itself to finding places for Jewish children to hide; in Belgium 50 percent of its Jewish population survived, and in Denmark, almost the entire Jewish population was saved.

The creativity, ingenuity, and courage of the resistance fighters and rescuers of the Holocaust, Jew and non-Jew alike, are now legend. They remind us of the responsibility all of us have to one another and they reaffirm the sanctity of life. They show us how courage, compassion, and kindness can change history. And finally, they are testimony to the fact that had resistance and rescue been more widespread, the Nazis could never have accomplished what they did. Had people individually and collectively refused to allow Hitler's "Final Solution," the Holocaust could never have happened. Perhaps, in the final analysis, these heroes and heroines will inspire us all to stand up for what is right—to make a difference in this world.

THROUGH THEIR EYES

TO "SAVE THE CHILDREN":
THE STORY OF JANUSZ KORCZAK

The story of Janusz Korczak tells of the selfless bravery of one man against the Nazis and how he worked to save hundreds of children during the Holocaust.

Korczak, born Henryk Goldszmit, grew up in Warsaw, Poland, where he was born in 1878 into an educated family. His grandfather was a doctor and his father was a lawyer. He adopted his pseudonym while a university student because he wanted to enter a literary competition and was afraid that his Jewish name would hurt his chances. Although he did not win the contest, his new name stuck.

Korczak chose to study medicine as a young man because he always wanted to help people. He began specializing in pediatrics and was an extremely popular doctor in the community because of his compassion for the poor children who lived in the slums of Warsaw. Korczak's popularity, however, went far beyond his own neighborhood. He was loved and respected throughout Poland, where people knew him as "The Old Doctor," the name he used for a radio program he did based on children and their education.

Korczak became particularly interested in the plight of the orphan child, which eventually led him to the founding of the Jewish Orphanage in Warsaw. Soon, his entire life was devoted to the orphanage, where he lived and worked 24 hours a day among his beloved children. Korczak's philosophy was that all children are basically good and if properly loved and cared for will grow up to be great achievers. He also believed that children had the right to govern themselves in the orphanage and could learn to properly discipline one another if necessary.

As the Jews of Warsaw were being forced into the large ghetto in 1939, Korczak insisted on remaining with his children and moved his orphanage into the ghetto. He could have safely hidden outside the ghetto with the aid of Christian friends, but he refused to abandon his more than 200 orphans. During the year that Korczak nurtured and watched over "his children" in the ghetto orphanage, he was aided by the cooperation of the ghetto Judenrat (Jewish leaders chosen to enforce

Nazi rule). The Judenrat protected Korczak and the children from the Nazis as much as they possibly could. However, by August 1942, even the ghetto leaders could no longer help Korczak, as the Nazis had ordered the few hundred remaining children in the Jewish Orphanage of the Warsaw Ghetto to be deported.

Korczak knew they were headed for the death camp of Treblinka but, rather than frighten them, he told the children to prepare for a picnic in the countryside. Although Korczak could have been saved and was begged by his admirers to let them help him, he chose to remain with his orphans, to shield them and be a comfort to them.

As Korczak and the children marched through the Warsaw Ghetto on their way to the train station, their departure was witnessed by a few hundred people. A diary kept by a noted historian of the Warsaw Ghetto, Emmanuel Ringelblum, and found after the war, described the scene:

> Korczak's Orphanage is to be evacuated today. Korczak himself can remain as physicians are needed. They are not marked for deportation and the Judenrat still possesses the power to protect him. As a matter of fact, he is safe but Korczak refuses to part with the children. He will not abandon his children; he will go with them...a long line was formed in front of the orphanage on Sliska Street. A long procession, children emaciated, weak, shriveled and shrunk...some have schoolbooks under their arms. No one is crying. Hitler's child-killers were seized by a mad fury and began firing their guns. More than 200 children stood quaking.

> Then something happened. They did not utter a cry, none made an attempt to run away, none sought to hide. Instead they nestled like wounded birdlings, around their teacher and protector, their father and brother Janusz Korczak. They were confident he would watch over them and protect his children with his emaciated body. The Nazi jackals showed no mercy. A pistol in one hand, whip in the other, they shouted at the children and ordered them to begin the march to the death trains....

> Cursed is the eye that beheld this horror! Janusz Korczak marches out front, hatless, carrying the youngest child. Behind him several nurses in white aprons, neat like children, marching to their slaughter, and on all sides are guards, Germans, Ukrainians, guns at ready! The very cobblestones wept...

source: Emmanuel Ringelblum, *Notes from the Warsaw Ghetto.*

This memorial was inspired by the courage and selfless bravery of Janusz Korczak. It stands at Yad Vashem in Jerusalem, Israel, in tribute to Korczak and the children of the Holocaust.

Reaching Beyond

1. What is your reaction to the scene described in Ringelblum's diary of Korczak and his children as they marched to the train station? What image affected you most?

2. Do you think Korczak should have told the children where they were going? Explain your answer.

3. Korczak had many opportunities to escape from the ghetto. Why was he so determined to stay with the children?

4. View one of the videos on Korczak's life (see Resources). What additional insights did the movie give you concerning Korczak and his commitment to his children?

THROUGH THEIR EYES

THE GHETTO FIGHTS BACK:
THE STORY OF MORDECAI ANIELEWICZ
(1919 or 1920–1943)

Mordecai Anielewicz, born into a poor family living in a Warsaw slum, rose to become one of the most revered of the Jewish resistance fighters, leading the Warsaw Ghetto Uprising.

In September, 1939, soon after the outbreak of World War II, Mordecai Anielewicz left his home in Warsaw to help establish a route for Jewish youth attempting to reach Palestine. Caught by the Soviets, he was put in jail. After he was released, Anielewicz returned to Warsaw briefly and then left for Vilna where he became part of a youth-led underground movement committed to educational and political activities against German occupation. Less than a year later, by January 1940, Anielewicz was a full-time underground activist in German-occupied Poland. Upon learning of the mass murder of Jews in the east after Germany invaded the Soviet Union in June 1941, Anielewicz began the creation of an organization that would help defend the ghetto.

By 1939, there were 400,000 Jews living in the approximately 3.5 square miles of the Warsaw Ghetto. They had their own newspapers, their own schools, and they tried to live their lives as normally as possible within a world turned upside down. After the mass deportation from Warsaw in the summer of 1942, only 60,000 Jews remained. Mordecai Anielewicz reorganized the small Zydowska Organizacja Bojowa (Jewish Fighting Organization, or ZOB) and they accomplished the unthinkable—they stole weapons from those on the other side of the ghetto, built an underground bunker, Mila 18 (made famous by Leon Uris), and plotted the Warsaw Ghetto Uprising. What makes the feats of the ZOB especially incredible is the fact that most of its fighters were girls and boys in their teens!

One of the first things the ZOB did was warn the ghetto residents that "resettlement" was a synonym for death. They urged people to flee and go into hiding, but their warnings fell on deaf ears. On January 19, 1943, the Germans suddenly began the next wave of mass deportation. Although caught off guard, members of the ZOB, with Anielewicz at the helm, joined the group of Jews being deported. The small group attacked the German guards, enabling the Jews to flee. This resistance halted the deportation for several months and gave the ghetto residents a sense of hope.

Finally, on April 19, 1943, the Germans began their final deportation of the Jews of the Warsaw Ghetto. By this time, the ZOB had increased its membership to 650 youths, divided into 22 fighting groups. Jews still in the ghetto dug tunnels and underground bunkers, laid mines, dug ditches, and bought dynamite. The Germans and Ukrainians circled the ghetto and 2,000 heavily armed SS men entered the main ghetto areas with tanks and all types of sophisticated weapons. The ZOB challenged the Germans and for three days a few hundred resistance fighters armed only with pistols fought in the streets against the German war machine. Retreating to the bunkers, this small army fought valiantly for almost four weeks, longer than the Polish resistance to the German invasion in September 1939, holding off the Nazi army and causing considerable losses. Finally, in a last effort to end the uprising, the Nazis torched the ghetto. The majority of those who survived the fires were deported. A very few, however, managed to escape into the woods, living to tell the story of the Warsaw Ghetto Uprising.

Mordecai Anielewicz died on May 8, 1943, at the age of 23, when his bunker at Mila 18 fell. However, he did not die in vain, for his dream of a Jewish resistance in the ghetto was realized. Anielewicz left a great legacy. He and his young resistance fighters showed how courage and determination, even in the face of overwhelming odds, can make a difference. And, in the end, Mordecai Anielewicz gave his people back their dignity and pride. Many of the survivors of the ghetto uprising immigrated to Israel where they established the Warsaw Ghetto Fighters House Kibbutz, a place of remembrance.

This memorial to Mordecai Anielewicz and the fighters of the Warsaw Ghetto Uprising stands in Warsaw, Poland.

Interestingly enough, in the city of Warsaw, there is little to commemorate what once was. Today, tall buildings stand overlooking the area that was the Warsaw Ghetto, the place where thousands lived, loved, and died. Yet, a single marker is placed over the area that once was Mila 18, and a statue of Anielewicz stands as a tribute to the courage of all who fight oppression.

Reaching Beyond

1. Why was it virtually impossible for those imprisoned in the ghetto to plan an uprising in the early years of the ghetto?

2. How do you explain the fact that a small army of untrained, poorly armed youths were able to hold off the Nazi soldiers for a period longer than the Polish resistance to the German invasion?

3. What is the legacy of uprisings such as that of the Warsaw Ghetto?

THROUGH THEIR EYES

THE DIARY: THE STORY OF PETR FISCHL

As told by Gabriel Dagan, in 1986, at the Ghetto Fighters House in Israel

In March 1939, the Nazis invaded Czechoslovakia and converted the small fortress town of Terezin, near the city of Prague, into a concentration camp. Although the Nazis said the concentration camp was a safe haven for Jews, it actually was a "holding place" where prisoners were kept until they could be transported to the death camp of Auschwitz. Terezin (Theresienstadt) Concentration Camp has often been called a "model ghetto" because it was here that the Nazis brought visiting dignitaries and the Red Cross.

After the first trains arrived at Terezin with entire families and children, the question of the care of the young people arose because this was not a death camp. It was decided to concentrate the children and youths in separate rooms, apart from their parents. Thus, it was up to the young people to develop their own little community in this imposed ghetto. All the youths over 14 had to work. They helped with gardening, and worked in the kitchen, bakery, and warehouses, attempting to lead some kind of normal existence even as the Nazis remained in terrifying command. And they lived in the shadow of daily transport to Auschwitz; the grim sounds of the railroad trains, arriving and departing with children each day, served as a constant reminder.

During the day, the children had a few free moments to pursue their hobbies and cultural interests. The Nazis knew they had quite a number of talented children and adults so they allowed them to organize plays, musicals, and lectures. Eventually, the organizers of the "prisoners" knew they could postpone their deportation if they continued to please the Nazis, who enjoyed the free entertainment. And the creative expression of the prisoners became a form of mental and spiritual resistance as it allowed them to "escape" their surroundings, if only for a few minutes.

One of the leaders of the children was Petr Fischl. Petr had always dreamed of being a writer, so he kept a diary. Every day he would write about everything he saw at Terezin. And, as he put his thoughts and feelings on paper, he kept himself spiritually alive. One day, Petr learned he had been selected for deportation on the next transport. He knew he might never return, so he passed his diary on to his friends. He instructed them that no matter who was selected for a transport, they were to keep passing the diary on so that eventually, one day, it would survive to tell the world what happened in Terezin.

Petr did survive Auschwitz and eventually immigrated to Israel. One day, about five years after the war, there was a single knock on the door of his home. When he answered it, a young woman his age asked, "Excuse me, are you Petr Fischl of Terezin?"

"I was— but not anymore, for I have taken an Israeli name now. My name is Gabriel Dagan," he replied.

"Well," she said, "I have something for you." She then handed him his precious well-worn diary and said, "Your diary was passed around from child to child and I ended up with it—I was told I must find you, so here it is!"

Gabriel Dagan (Petr Fischl) retells his story to many people. An excerpt from his diary appears in the book ...*I Never Saw Another Butterfly...Children's Drawings and Poems from Terezin Concentration Camp, 1942–1944.* The note below his entry states that Petr perished in Auschwitz in 1944. Today he says, "A part of me did perish."

A total of 15,000 children under the age of 15 passed though the concentration camp at Terezin. One hundred survived.

Reaching Beyond

1. How did Terezin differ from other concentration camps? Why did the Nazis allow a camp such as Terezin to exist?

2. Why are the children's diaries, drawings, and poems considered a form of spiritual resistance?

3. What did Petr Fischl mean when he said, "A part of me did perish"?

4. Read ...*I Never Saw Another Butterfly...* (Part II of this book contains a section dedicated to this collection of poems and drawings by the children of Terezin).

THROUGH THEIR EYES

HANNAH SZENES—MISSION: RESCUE

Hannah Szenes was born in 1921 in the city of Budapest, Hungary, into a literary and artistic world. Her early years could hardly have prepared her for life after the Nazi invasion or for the incredible feats of heroism that have made her name synonymous with courage.

Hannah Szenes' world was first turned upside down at the age of six, when her father, the famous playwright Bela Szenes, died. His death left a huge void in her life. She resolved to "make a difference in the world," and silently promised both him and herself that she would one day be a great person.

Hannah's first experiences with anti-Semitism came when she attended a Protestant school at age 13 and was charged three times the tuition of the non-Jewish students. As news of riots in Germany and of the laws being passed against Jews spread, Hannah began to witness more and more incidents of anti-Semitic behavior. By the summer of 1937, Jews and Christians were segregated and Hannah could no longer associate with her non-Jewish friends and was restricted from most public places.

As the Jewish people became more and more discriminated against, Hannah began a personal quest to learn the history of her people. She read about the persecution of Jews since Biblical times and through her studies discovered Theodore Herzl, a Jew born in Budapest. From Herzl's work, she learned about Zionism, which professed that all Jews dispersed throughout the world should return to Zion (Palestine), the homeland of the Jews. This, too, became Hannah's personal quest. After graduating from school with honors, Hannah was accepted to the School of Agriculture in the town of Nahalal, in the northern part of the land now called Israel. There, Hannah had to adjust to a new culture, a new language, and learn to survive on her own—she loved every minute of it! But her newly found happiness was clouded by the news coming from Europe about the destruction of the Jews. Daily, she worried about her mother in Budapest, and her brother, George, who was living in Nazi-occupied France. In the diary she kept, she reflected on the fact that she felt she was an emissary entrusted with a mission. However, what this mission would be was yet unclear to her.

By 1942, Hannah had little success in gaining asylum for her mother. The British, who governed Palestine, had restructured Jewish immigration, greatly reducing the number of people allowed to enter the land. In 1943, Hannah became convinced that she must do something to rescue not only her mother but other Jews in Hungary. She enlisted in the Haganah (the Israeli Underground) and, in 1944, left for Egypt for special training. Hannah was one of five selected for a most dangerous mission—to parachute into Hungary to find and open escape routes for British pilots. The plan was to parachute into Yugoslavia and eventually move into Hungary. Their lives constantly threatened, Hannah and her companions relayed important information to the Resistance Movement, resulting in the rescue of Jewish and British soldiers.

The more Hannah learned of the atrocities and horrors faced by her fellow Hungarian Jews, the more determined she was to reach Hungary as quickly as possible, despite the risks. Soon after she crossed the border, Hannah was caught by the Hungarian police. She was beaten and questioned relentlessly about her mission. Finally declared an enemy of Hungary, a spy and a traitor, Hannah was imprisoned in Budapest, stripped naked, chained, tortured, and beaten. Finally, she relented and gave her captors one piece of information, "My name is Hannah Szenes."

On October 28, 1944, Hannah was put on trial for high treason. Hannah gave an impassioned speech explaining that she was not a traitor but that her country had betrayed her by acts of discrimination and racism that forced her to leave and live elsewhere. So shocked were the judges after listening to her words that a verdict could not immediately be reached and she was sent back to prison. Finally, Hannah was told that she had been sentenced to death with no right to appeal. Within a few hours, Hannah faced the firing squad. She was strapped to a post, and, refusing a blindfold, stared at the sky ahead, dying with dignity. She was 23 years old.

Hannah's mother Catherine survived the Nazi death machine by hiding in a convent. Her brother eventually reached Palestine. Hannah, too, reached Israel, for she is buried in Jerusalem. On the headstone of her grave is the carving of a parachute. Throughout Israel, to this day, the name of Hannah Szenes is legend, inspiring the young to the great deeds that can be accomplished.

Reaching Beyond

1. People react to adversity and tragedy in different ways. How did the death of her father affect Hannah's future accomplishments?

2. What qualities led Hannah Szenes to leave the safety of Israel and parachute into Eastern Europe, risking her life to save others?

3. If Hannah were living today, what advice might she give to people your age about the responsibilities we have to one another?

4. For more information on the life of Hannah Szenes, read *Hannah Szenes—A Song of Light* by Maxine Schur (see the accompanying unit in Part II) or *In Kindling Flame: The Story of Hannah Senesh 1921–1944* by Linda Atkinson. (Senesh is an Americanized spelling of Hannah's last name.)

THROUGH THEIR EYES

RAOUL WALLENBERG: A LEGEND OF HEROISM

Could one individual actually have made a difference and rescued thousands of people from certain death at the hands of the Nazis? The answer is "yes." That individual's name is Raoul Wallenberg.

Who was he? Where did he come from? How did he do it? What happened to him? These are the usual questions asked by anyone who has ever heard the unusual story of the "lost hero," Raoul Wallenberg, who saved tens of thousands of Jews in Hungary in 1944.

Raoul Wallenberg was the son of a Swedish naval officer. He attended the finest military schools and even studied architecture in the United States, at the University of Michigan. After working in South Africa and in Israel, Raoul returned to Sweden, where he became more and more concerned about the plight of the Jews in Europe. Established as a successful businessman in Sweden, a neutral country during the war, Wallenberg was offered the opportunity of helping the Hungarian Jews and he readily accepted the challenge.

The year 1944 was a turning point for the Jews in Hungary. The Nazi government demanded the Hungarian government turn over for deportation the remaining 800,000 Jews living in Hungary. Despite the efforts of the puppet government in Hungary led by Admiral Nicolas Horthy, 435,000 Jews from the provinces were sent to their deaths at Auschwitz. In the meantime, Adolf Eichmann set in motion plans to deport the remaining 230,000 Jews living in Budapest, the capital city of Hungary.

Into this arena of death came Raoul Wallenberg, named special envoy with diplomatic protection. Armed with little more than sheer determination and fortified with courage, Wallenberg set up his own headquarters at the Swedish Embassy and created special passports with the Swedish seal, granting immunity to those who held them. Although these passports had no real validity, they looked authentic enough to the German and Hungarian officials, whose attention was diverted to the German losses in the war and who were worried about postwar reprisals. Volunteer Jews worked relentlessly around the clock producing more and more of these counterfeit passports. In addition to distributing as many passports as possible, Wallenberg established shelters and "safe houses" where Jews could live under Swedish protection.

The successful efforts to rescue the Jews of Hungary and resist Nazi domination made Adolf Eichmann even more determined to destroy the remaining Jews in Budapest. He established the Arrow Cross Government and replaced Admiral Horthy with Ferenc Szalasi. With the Arrow Cross in power, the documents Wallenberg distributed were not recognized. Jews began disappearing and a new reign of terror began in force. Wallenberg intervened by appealing to the wife of the Minister of Foreign Affairs, threatening to expose her Jewish heritage and reminding her that German defeat was imminent. Once more, the almost 20,000 Jews holding documents found protection. However, more than 200,000 Jews were still without papers and Eichmann decided it was time to round up these remaining Jews for a death march.

In freezing rain, 27,000 people were marched from Budapest to trains bound for death camps. They marched 20–25 miles a day. In the midst of this horror, Wallenberg appeared at the side of the Jews, riding up and down, distributing food, medicine, and clothing, and filling in blank passports for people whose release he later demanded. In this manner alone, he saved an additional 2,000 men, women, and children.

In December 1944, the Russians entered Hungary. But Wallenberg was nowhere to be found—he had disappeared into the night. Survivors searched for him, wishing to communicate their gratitude, but to no avail. Rumor placed him in Russia and there were reports that he was being held as an ally of the Germans. Wallenberg's fate has never been verified, but in 1957, a Russian report said that he died in prison there in 1947. To this day, rumors circulate that he is alive, imprisoned somewhere in Russia.

At the end of the war, over 144,000 Jews had survived in Budapest. While half of Hungary's Jews had been killed, those who survived owe their lives, in large measure, to the efforts of one man—Raoul Wallenberg.

Reaching Beyond

1. What dangers did Wallenberg encounter in his work to rescue the Jews of Hungary? Be specific.

2. If Wallenberg were discovered alive today, what do you think he would say about his incredible mission in Hungary and his accomplishments?

3. How would you respond to the question "But what can only one person do?"

4. If you would like to learn more about Raoul Wallenberg and his work to rescue the Jews, read Elenore Lester's *Wallenberg: The Man in the Iron Web* (Prentice-Hall, 1982) or John Bierman's *Righteous Gentile: The Story of Raoul Wallenberg, Missing Hero of the Holocaust* (Viking, 1981).

RESISTANCE AND RESCUE:
THE HEROES AND HEROINES OF THE HOLOCAUST

REFLECTIONS

1. What types of resistance were described in the stories in this chapter? Of all these forms of resistance, which do you feel is most difficult? Explain.

2. What qualities did the rescuers you read about seem to have in common?

3. When rescuers and resistance fighters were asked why they risked their lives, they usually responded with, "Because it was the right thing to do." What does this say to you?

4. Explain this quote from the Talmud (the collection of writings constituting the Jewish civil and religious law): "Whoever saves a single soul, it is as if he had saved the whole world."

5. What if the acts of resistance and rescue you read about were more the rule than the exception during World War II? How might history have been changed?

6. A special avenue leading to the Holocaust Museum in Israel is lined with carob trees. This special area is called the "Avenue of the Righteous," and each tree in it has been planted to remember a non-Jew who risked his/her life for Jews. By 1986, over 16,000 trees had been planted on the avenue or on the hillside beyond it. In addition to being a very special way to remember the accomplishments of these people, why is this tribute so significant for the world to see?

EXTENSIONS

1. Read excerpts from *Rescue: The Story of How Gentiles Saved Jews in the Holocaust* by Milton Meltzer or similar books (listed in the Resource section of this book). Select a favorite story of rescue or resistance and retell it through the creation of a mural, through dramatic interpretation, or through the words of a song or ballad.

2. Summarize and illustrate your favorite story of rescue or resistance (see Activity 1 above). Compile class summaries into an anthology that can be kept in your school's library.

3. Many stories of rescue and resistance focus on the remarkable heroic deeds of individuals. However, there were instances during the Holocaust in which an entire village, such as Le Chambon, came together to save its Jewish neighbors. And, in one instance, an entire nation fought to rescue its Jewish citizens. Through your reading, discover how the people of Denmark protected its entire Jewish population. Select one or more specific acts of defiance against the Nazis and write (and perform) a play that recreates the effort and spirit of resistance/rescue.

4. Just as individuals and groups exhibited the courage to defy the Nazis and protect Jewish men, women, and children during World War II, there are those who show similar courage today by doing what they believe is right even if it is not the popular thing to do. Create a class bulletin board of articles from newspapers and magazines that describe acts of courage you admire. Select the act of courage you find most amazing and write an essay to accompany the article that expresses your feelings about the situation. Create an interesting (and inspiring) caption for the bulletin board.

5. If you were to teach another class about the lessons of resistance and rescue, what would you do? With a group of students, design such a lesson and teach it to another class in your school.

CHAPTER 5

Prejudice, Stereotypes, and Scapegoats

"Evil does not prevail until it is given power."

The Zohar

PREJUDICE, STEREOTYPES, AND SCAPEGOATS

From every corner of our world, we hear reports of racial violence. No group seems to be exempt. Violence, prejudice, and discrimination aimed at one group or another is rampant. This prejudice and discrimination has its roots in the beginning of humankind, and its branches have become so widespread that they have extended into the heart of the twentieth century. These branches have woven a web of hate so strong that it created a Holocaust in which an entire people, an entire culture, was virtually destroyed.

Prejudice is defined as an attitude toward all members of a particular group. It is usually unfavorable, formed from ignorance, and often results in intolerance at best, hatred and violence at worst. The Jewish people, as a group, have a long tradition of facing discrimination and persecution. From early times, they were regarded as a threat because they would not accept Christianity. Crusaders, on their quests to the Holy Land, murdered Jews. The Jewish people were expelled from England, France, Italy, the German states, and Spain between the thirteenth and sixteenth centuries.

The Jewish people had no homeland of their own. They were often considered "foreigners" in the countries in which they lived, and as such were resented. They were generally not allowed to own land and had to develop skills in merchandising. Many of them became merchants, money lenders, and traders—the only work from which they were not prohibited. Yet, their sense of obligation, their work ethic, their sense of responsibility, and their perseverance led them, despite the discrimination, to achieve.

Fifty years after the Holocaust, anti-Semitism still exists in Poland. Anti-Semitic slogans were scrawled on the walls of one of the few existing synagogues in Warsaw, Poland, in April 1992, when the city was visited by over 5,000 Jewish teens from all over the world.

The growth of anti-Semitism was in direct proportion to the economic success of the Jewish people. Politically, the Jewish people emerged as a capitalist class which aroused hatred from the other more conservative groups. According to a theory of the late nineteenth century, the Jewish people had become more than the religious group that they were. Despite the fact that the Jewish people had made incredible humanitarian contributions, were known for their scholarly teachings and their love for peace, they were looked upon as inferior. Stereotypes of the Jewish people emerged—all Jews looked a certain way, acted a certain way, and so forth—despite the fact that Jewish people were as different as the cultures in which they lived.

The Nazis measured the heads of the Jewish prisoners in an attempt to find physical differences between them and the pure Aryan race they were trying to create.

Because of this history of prejudice, it was easy for the Nazi propaganda machine to blame the economic and social ills facing post-World War I Germany on the Jewish people. Throughout history people have always sought a *scapegoat*, a person or group of people to blame for the actions of others. The word itself comes from ancient times in which a goat was let loose in the wilderness after the priest had placed the sins of the people upon it. In this way, the people were blameless, no longer responsible for their own actions. The Jewish people became the Nazi scapegoat, the scapegoat for all those who were less than successful. It was easier to find a scapegoat than to try to find and implement realistic solutions to the problems affecting them.

Prejudice, and the resulting stereotypes and scapegoating, helps no one and hurts everyone. It is a virus that eats away at our very beings. It is a cancer that destroys the spirit and kills the soul. But, like a virus or a cancer, prejudice can be destroyed. Education is the best cure.

Today's society is filled with propaganda dedicated to molding perceptions and attitudes. This propaganda does not exist simply to sell breakfast foods and cars. It is carefully twisted and shaped by certain well-organized groups to encourage hate and violence. We can and must stand up and speak out against prejudice and discrimination. We must learn to look beyond the words. We must learn to think critically, explore issues, analyze purposes, and draw our own conclusions based on the facts and not the preconceived ideas that have been perpetuated based on ignorance and fear.

Prejudice and its consequences will continue until we work together to understand, accept, and even appreciate the differences that exist among people. It can happen, and it starts with just one person.

The Nazis used every means to dehumanize the Jewish people. They even went so far as to destroy Jewish cemeteries.

PREJUDICE, STEREOTYPES, AND SCAPEGOATS

REFLECTIONS

1. Define *prejudice, stereotypes,* and *scapegoats.* Discuss examples of each in today's society.

2. Why is prejudice so widespread?

3. Why is prejudice so dangerous? Over the course of history, what groups have been victims of prejudice? What happened as a result of this prejudice?

4. Discuss propaganda techniques that have been and are still used to perpetuate prejudice against people of different ethnic, religious, and social groups? What can be done to make these propaganda techniques ineffective?

5. Think about the prejudices you have formed over the years. Where did these prejudices originate? What can *you* do to eliminate them?

EXTENSIONS

1. Look at prejudice in a different way by completing the following:
   If prejudice were an animal, what animal would it be? Why?
   If prejudice were a food, what food would it be? Why?
   If prejudice were a number, what number would it be? Why?
   If prejudice were a shape, what shape would it be? Why?
   Create a picture of prejudice by using the images suggested by your responses to the above questions. Share your picture with your classmates and display it.

2. Become prejudice. Write a story about your life. Explain what you look like, how you influence people, and how you are responsible for specific situations. Also, discuss what can be done to eliminate you.

3. Find articles in current magazines and newspapers that describe instances of prejudice. Lead a class discussion of the article. In your discussion, try to determine why the prejudice exists and what students can do to help bring about public awareness of the problem and work to eliminate it.

4. With classmates, compile a list of organizations that work to eliminate prejudice and discrimination, such as the American Civil Liberties Union (ACLU), the National Association for the Advancement of Colored People (NAACP), and the National Conference of Christians and Jews (NCCJ). Write a letter to one of these organizations to learn more about the nature of prejudice and to discover what the organization is doing to eliminate it.

5. Elie Wiesel, a Holocaust survivor and author of *Night*, wrote, "Whoever hates, hates his brother, and whenever one hates his brother, one always hates himself." Write an essay on what this quotation means to you. Create a poster with captions that reflect your feelings about prejudice and discrimination.

CHAPTER 6

To Heal the World: Ethical Issues

"How wonderful it is that nobody need wait a single moment before starting to improve the world."

Anne Frank

HISTORICAL NOTES

TO HEAL THE WORLD: ETHICAL ISSUES

"Some are guilty, all are responsible."
From the Yom HaShoah Service
(in memory of the Holocaust)

The conscience of the world must be awakened to the hatred and bigotry that exists—a hatred so strong that it could bring about the Holocaust, the death of six million men, women, and children. The Holocaust reminds us of what human beings are capable of doing to other human beings when prejudice and discrimination are unleashed. It reminds us of what can happen when people stand by and watch it happen—allow it to happen.

Survivors of the Holocaust want their history told so that new light will shine with truth, covering the "dark sun of Auschwitz" and other death camps. The stories of the Holocaust are being passed to a new generation to be remembered for generations to come. They remind us that we must never allow this to happen again to any people, anywhere. If the victims who perished could speak today, they would say, "Don't let the world forget us and why we died." And we should be able to say, "We have not forgotten—your voices are not stilled." The Holocaust reminds us and we must remember.

The society of human beings in Eastern Europe in the 1940s reached its lowest level of civilized behavior by allowing a nation and culture of people to be eradicated from the face of the earth because it was "ethnically different" and a minority. However, the term *ethnic cleansing* probably sounds familiar today, over 50 years later, as brother fights brother in different parts of the world, in places such as Bosnia (in the former Yugoslavia) and in Rwanda (in east-central Africa). Racism is America's deepest wound. Hate groups are on the rise, promising a deeper commitment to ethnic cleansing and purification.

We must, in turn, make a deeper commitment to confront the issues raised by the Holocaust—issues of discrimination, prejudice, and hate—which are still dominating the hearts and minds of people around the world. We can no longer stand back, hear the news, shake our heads in disbelief, and go on with our own lives. We must ask questions, ask more questions, call attention to the issues, and formulate workable solutions to turn prejudice into understanding, discrimination into tolerance, and hate into acceptance.

The Holocaust reminds us of certain universal principles and ethical issues that need to be internalized if we are to "heal the world." First, we must confront those who promote bigotry and racism. We must teach that everyone can live in peace and harmony if we recognize that all people have a right to live their lives, free from persecution. Ours is a world of changes and choices—a multicultural world. Immigrants come to our shores daily, fleeing poverty and oppression. We must tear down the artificial boundaries of intolerance and together build a nation as dynamic as our individual and cultural differences and as strong as the commonalties which bind us together as members of the human race. Second, we must learn and teach our own children, from an early age, that one cannot be an apathetic bystander. Silence in the face of evil is a collaboration. The problems of others must become our problems if we are to find solutions.

"The Ethical Issues of Teaching the Holocaust" advanced by the scholars at Yad Vashem, the central authority on the Holocaust in Jerusalem, Israel, suggest three commandments to further the study of Holocaust education. These same commandments can and should provide the framework for ethical education in general: " Thou shalt not be a perpetrator," "Thou shalt not be a bystander," "Thou shalt not be a victim." With these commandments to guide our thoughts and actions, it will be difficult for those who discriminate, for those who hate, to be successful in their war against humanity.

TO HEAL THE WORLD:
ETHICAL ISSUES

REFLECTIONS

1. What is meant by the words *perpetrator, bystander*, and *victim*, which are used in the commandments adopted by the scholars at Yad Vashem to teach the ethical issues of the Holocaust? Discuss a time when you or someone you know was either a perpetrator, a bystander, or a victim. How did the situation make you feel?

2. How can we become more sensitive to the feelings and conditions of others?

3. An ability to feel empathy for others was identified as being one of the most important factors in determining why one person would stand up for another who is being discriminated against. How can we develop empathy, in ourselves and others, to the plights of those who are facing discrimination and prejudice?

4. Do you believe it is possible for another Holocaust to happen again in our country or in another? Explain.

EXTENSIONS

1. With a group of other students, create a dilemma based on a current issue facing our world. Involve others in discussing this dilemma using the steps outlined in Extension Activity #5.

2. Think of a situation currently unfolding in your school or community in which you could possibly be a perpetrator, a bystander, or a victim. What can you do to ensure that you do not take on any of these three roles? Develop a plan of action.

3. Lead a discussion with others based on the meaning behind the words "Some are guilty, all are responsible." Encourage those in your group to discuss instances throughout history in which this concept would hold true. Discuss how those who were responsible could have acted differently and how history might have been changed. Select one of these events and rewrite history.

4. Write an essay on the topic of individual responsibility in the face of choices that we must make throughout our lives.

5. Read the following dilemma (one which was faced by people throughout Europe during World War II) and with your classmates become involved in a discussion of the dilemma by following the steps that are listed below it:

SHULTZ'S DILEMMA

During the late 1930s and early 1940s, Germany invaded and conquered Austria, Poland, France, the Netherlands, Norway, and Denmark. Throughout these countries and in Germany, the Jewish people were routinely forced into ghettos and later transported to concentration camps and killed. This was known as Hitler's "Final Solution." By the time the war had ended, over six million Jewish men, women, and children had been killed.

Living in Germany at this time were two families who had been friends for six years, ever since their oldest children had been born. The Rosen family was Jewish; their friends the Schultzes were not. Both families knew what was being done to the Jewish people, and the Rosens decided that they had to escape from Germany if they were to survive.

The Rosens, along with other Jewish families, tried to develop a plan of action that would lead them to safety; but they soon realized that no matter what they did, they would be discovered. The trains and all other forms of transportation were guarded by the Nazi soldiers. All routes out of their city were blocked. Time was running out. Already many of their friends had been rounded up in the middle of the night, never to be heard from again.

Finally, the Rosens had an idea, the only one they felt had a chance of working. In the middle of the night, they dressed their young children, Stephen, age six, Adam, age four, and the baby, Rachel, who was two years old—and quietly left their home. In the shadows, they made their way to the Schultz home and knocked at the door. They begged the Schultzes to hide them in the basement of their house, knowing the Schultzes were the only ones they could trust.

Mr. Schultz and his wife knew they had to make a decision. If they allowed the Rosens to stay with them, they risked death for themselves and their own children. The Nazi soldiers were ordered to shoot on sight anyone found aiding a Jewish person. They had witnessed such an execution only a few weeks ago. On the other hand, they knew that if they did not help their friends, the Rosens would be transported to concentration camps and meet certain death. They looked at the faces of the Rosen children, so young and innocent. Then they thought of their own children tucked safely in bed.

Steps to discussing the dilemma:

a. Clarify the facts of the dilemma, the "who," "what," "where," "why," and "how."

b. Write an individual statement of what you believe Mr. and Mrs. Schultz should do and list the three reasons you believe are most important in arriving at this decision.

c. Get into groups with other students who have made the same decision. As a group, select the three best reasons to support your choice.

d. Discuss the dilemma with the entire class—each group should explain its position and accompanying reasons.

e. Rewrite your individual statement of what you believe Mr. and Mrs. Schultz should do. Again give your three best reasons.

f. Discuss the following: Did your ideas change? If so, what do you think helped cause this change? If not, what helped you become even more firm in your decision?

PART 2
THE LITERATURE OF THE HOLOCAUST

As the Russian armies approached, the Nazis destroyed Treblinka Death Camp in an attempt to wipe out any evidence of their "Final Solution." Today, in the area that was Treblinka, stone monuments stand to remind us of those people who were killed. The literature of the Holocaust is also a monument reminding us of the Holocaust. It allows us to hear the voices of the victims.

THE LITERATURE OF THE HOLOCAUST

Individual and Group Responsibility 75

Terrible Things
(upper elementary through high school)

Number the Stars
(upper elementary and middle school)

Resistance and Rescue 82

The Island on Bird Street
(upper elementary through high school)

Hannah Szenes: A Song of Light
(middle school and high school)

The Short Life of Sophie Scholl
(high school)

Voices of the Holocaust 94

Daniel's Story
(upper elementary and middle school)

The Devil's Arithmetic
(upper elementary and middle school)

Alicia: My Story
(middle school and high school)

Anne Frank: The Diary of a Young Girl and
Anne Frank: Beyond the Diary
(middle school and high school)

Night
(middle school and high school)

Poetry, Art, and Photography From the Holocaust.................................115

...I Never Saw Another Butterfly...
(upper elementary through high school)

The Children We Remember
(upper elementary through high school)

Terrible Things: An Allegory of the Holocaust

Bunting, Eve. *Terrible Things: An Allegory of the Holocaust.* Philadelphia: The Jewish Publication Society, 1989. Illustrated by Stephen Gammell.

ABOUT THE AUTHOR

Eve Bunting spent her childhood in the small town of Maghera, County Derry, in Northern Ireland, the town of her birth. Her father was the postmaster and owned a produce shop. After graduating from Methodist College in Belfast, Bunting met her husband and nine years later, in 1960, they journeyed across the ocean and settled in San Francisco and later Pasadena, California, with their three young children.

While Bunting never planned on being an author, her education in Ireland encouraged her writing talents. Her first book was published in 1972, when she was 43 years old. Since that time she has authored more than 100 books for children. For her, writing is as natural as breathing and she gets her ideas from the world around her. She strives to use messages that are special to her in her books.

SUMMARY

First the Terrible Things came for creatures with feathers on their backs. And, while the other creatures of the woods watched, the birds who had shared their lives in the woods disappeared. With each visit, the Terrible Things took another type of creature—nothing stopped them. Little Rabbit questioned their motives and wanted to do something to stop the Terrible Things, but his father told him repeatedly to mind his own business. Gradually, each type of creature that inhabited the woods is taken away except the rabbits, but now there is no one to come to their rescue.

Terrible Things: *An Allegory of the Holocaust* presents students with a picture of what happens when one does not stand up against evil. While nothing can ever compare with the incomprehensible tragedy of the Holocaust, the book presents perhaps the most important message of the Holocaust to its readers—stand up for what you think is right, whether or not you are personally affected by what is happening. In this way, the Terrible Things will never claim another victim.

VOCABULARY

allegory: a story in which people, things, and happenings have another meaning; allegories are used for teaching or explaining.

concentration camps: a group of labor and death camps built by the Nazis for Jews and other "undesirables."

Nazis: acronym for the National Socialist German Workers' Party—headed by Hitler—whose major goal was to annihilate the Jewish people.

Encourage students to study the cover of *Terrible Things: An Allegory of the Holocaust.*

Have them make predictions about the content of the book, based on the title, subtitle, and illustrations. Discuss what is meant by the word *allegory*.

QUESTIONS AND ANSWERS

1. How did the animals in the woods get along before the Terrible Things entered their lives? (They shared the woods in peace. They were content.)

2. How did the animals in the woods react to the Terrible Things when they first came for the creatures with feathers on their backs? (Most were relieved that they did not have feathers.)

3. How did the animals rationalize the selections made by the Terrible Things? (They created reasons for the animals being taken away. The birds were too noisy; the squirrels were greedy; frogs were lumpy and slimy; the porcupines were bad-tempered.)

4. How does Little Rabbit's father respond to Little Rabbit's question "Why did the Terrible Things want the birds?" (His father told him not to question the selection and just be grateful that the Terrible Things had not come for them.)

5. What were his father's reasons for disagreeing with Little Rabbit when he suggested that they leave the woods because the Terrible Things might return. (His father said that the woods had always been their home and he believed that the Terrible Things would not come back for them.)

DISCUSSION TOPICS

1. What were the Terrible Things?

2. Why is the book considered an allegory to the Holocaust? Do you agree? Why or why not?

3. Of all the animals in the forest, which was the wisest? Explain.

4. Why didn't the animals in the woods band together to resist the Terrible Things?

5. Preceding the story, the author, Eve Bunting, included a brief introduction. Read this introduction carefully, and after reading the book, discuss the terrible things she alludes to that can happen today if we take the easy way out and look the other way.

1. Look at the pictures of the Terrible Things. What do you see? Describe the Terrible Things.

2. List the terrible things facing our world today. Select one and describe what you can do to prevent it from happening.

3. Imagine that you are Little Rabbit. Create a journal entry to describe what has happened to your family and friends, the reasons why such a terrible thing could have happened, etc.

4. Describe the woods with all the animals living together in harmony. Then, describe the woods with only White Rabbit left in it. What is wrong with this second picture? Why is diversity so important?

5. Based on your study of the Holocaust, explore and express your reactions to this book as an allegory to the Holocaust.

EXTENSIONS

1. Create a sign that Little Rabbit might have left in the woods to warn others about the Terrible Things.

2. Write your own introduction to the book geared to students your age. Send your class' best introduction to the publisher of *Terrible Things*. Suggest that they might use it in future editions or in their marketing strategy.

3. Read *Terrible Things: An Allegory of the Holocaust* to other students. Lead a discussion that helps them understand a fundamental lesson of the Holocaust—the need to stand up against evil and work together so that terrible things cannot happen to others.

4. Create a short story that might also be considered an allegory to teach the lessons of the Holocaust.

5. Make a list of the terrible things threatening our lives and times (See Writing Activity # 2). In small groups, select one terrible thing. Research it, create several options for alleviating the problem, and from these options select the one you believe is most viable (possible). Create a campaign to make others aware of this terrible thing and what they can do to prevent it from happening.

Number the Stars

Lowry, Lois. *Number the Stars.* Boston: Houghton Mifflin Co., 1989.

ABOUT THE AUTHOR

Born in Honolulu, Hawaii, March 20, 1937, Lois Lowry decided at a very young age to become a writer—she was only four years old! She could never have imagined the impression her books would have upon the readers and the honors her books would receive. From her Anastasia Krupnik books to her Newbery Award-winning books, *Number the Stars* (1990) and *The Giver* (1994), Lois Lowry's stories have become favorites of children and adolescents. Her topics range from the serious to the humorous, from stories of war and the death of a sibling to those that depict the humorous adventures of a young girl. Lowry's stories are filled with emotion and an understanding of human nature. Many of her own childhood experiences have inspired her writing. For example, Lowry's own sister died when Lowry was 25. She had to deal with the loss just as her character Meg did when she realized that her sister was dying in the book *A Summer to Die.*

Speaking to a group of teachers and librarians, Lois Lowry was once asked her purpose in writing books for adolescents. Her reply—"to make a reader feel less alone..."

SUMMARY

Based on the historical events of Nazi-occupied Denmark in the 1940s, *Number the Stars* describes the Danish Resistance and its successful efforts to save the Jewish population of Denmark—nearly 7,000 men, women, and children. The story of the courage of an entire nation is depicted through the friendship between two families, one Jewish, one Christian. Annemarie's family members risk their own lives to hide her best friend, Ellen, from the Nazi soldiers and later smuggle Ellen, her parents, and many others across the sea to freedom in Sweden. Through this story of courage and determination, we learn about individual responsibility as well as group responsibility, as the people of Denmark stand up to evil to rescue their friends and neighbors.

VOCABULARY

De Frie Danske—The Free Danes: an illegal newspaper that described the efforts of the Danish Resistance.

PREREADING
ACTIVITY With students, locate the countries of Denmark, Norway, and Sweden on a world map. What countries, bodies of water, etc., border these lands? What is their distance from Germany? What natural boundaries do they possess?

**QUESTIONS
AND
ANSWERS**

1. Why did Denmark destroy its own navy? (So that the Nazis could not use it for their own purposes.)

2. Why did Denmark surrender to Germany without putting up a fight? (The country was small and undefended, with a very small army. The people would have been destroyed if they had tried to defend themselves against the Nazi forces.)

3. How did the powder in the handkerchief keep the dogs from discovering the hidden passengers in the boats taking them to safety in Sweden? (The powder in the handkerchief was composed of rabbit's blood and cocaine. The blood attracted the dogs and as they sniffed the cocaine it deadened their sense of smell.)

4. Why were so many Jewish citizens transported to Sweden? (Sweden still remained free from Nazi invasion.)

5. Why did so few Jewish people die at the hands of the Nazis in Denmark compared to the number killed in the rest of Europe? (The population of Denmark saw the Jewish people as fellow citizens. They rallied together to protect their brothers and sisters.)

**DISCUSSION
TOPICS**

1. Although, technically, Denmark surrendered to Germany in 1940, discuss how the people really never actually surrendered. Cite specific examples from the book.

2. Agree or disagree with Annemarie's statement, "All of Denmark must be bodyguard for the Jews." How might history have been different if people in all countries had had this same sense of responsibility?

3. What is the significance of the book's title, *Number the Stars*. (The verse on pages 86-87 of *Number the Stars* may help you respond to this question.)

4. Annemarie and Uncle Henrik discuss the meaning of the word *brave*. What is your definition of this term? Discuss instances of bravery that you have witnessed in your life.

5. How did Denmark's King Christian set an example of courage and resistance for all his people?

1. Take the point of view of one of the members of Annemarie's family. Write a simulated journal entry in which you explain why you are risking your life to save the lives of others.

2. Lois Lowry, in the book's afterword, includes a paragraph written by a young Resistance leader, Kim Malthe-Bruun, to his mother, shortly before he was put to death by the Nazis. Read this paragraph and then write a journal entry that expresses your ideal of human decency.

3. What one incident in the book affected you most? Explain the event and your reaction to it.

4. Select one of the efforts of the Danish Resistance and write a newspaper article for *De Frie Danske (The Free Danes)* describing what happened and its significance to the cause. Put your article together with others to create an issue of this important publication.

5. Select a favorite character from the book *Number the Stars*. With this character in mind, respond to the following in as many different ways as you can:

   Example: If I were Annemarie, I would wonder if I would ever see Ellen again.

   If I were _____ (name of character), I would _____.

   If I were _____ (same character), I would _____.

   If I were _____ (same character), I would _____.

   (You may repeat this as many more times as you wish—but the minimum number of times is three.)

EXTENSIONS

1. Divide into groups, one group per country, and locate significant facts about the Scandinavian countries of Denmark, Norway, and Sweden and their involvement in the events of World War II and the Holocaust. Create a chart listing the information you uncovered and share this with your class. What similarities and differences can you find between life in these countries and their people and life in Eastern Europe and its people?

2. Throughout history, there have been those who risked their lives to save others. Research other such efforts such as the Underground Railroad (the organization to bring slaves to freedom in the North) and the U.N. peace-keeping forces in Somalia. Select a favorite effort made by one such group—summarize it and create an illustration to accompany it. Display your summary and picture along with others in your class on a bulletin board with a fitting title, such as "Resistance Is..."

3. The top scientists of Denmark came up with the idea of filling a handkerchief with a mixture of rabbit's blood and cocaine so that the Nazis' dogs were unable to sniff out passengers hidden in boats bound for Sweden. Research this and other efforts of the Danish Resistance. With a group of students, retell one of your favorite stories of resistance.

4. Every country, most religions, and most organizations have logos or symbols to represent them. The United States has its stars and stripes. The Red Cross has its red cross on a background of white. Create a symbol or emblem to represent the need for understanding between and among people of all lands, races, and religions. Share your symbol with your class and explain its significance.

5. With classmates, listen to and record the words to the song "We Are the World," recorded in the late 1980s by popular recording stars, actors, and actresses to call attention to the needs of children all over the world. Use this song as a model to create an anthem to fight prejudice and teach acceptance and tolerance. Teach this song to others in your school.

The Island on Bird Street

Orlev, Uri. *The Island on Bird Street.* New York: Houghton Mifflin Co., 1984 (originally published in 1981).

ABOUT THE AUTHOR

Uri Orlev was born Jerzy Orlowski in Warsaw, Poland, in 1931. He spent the first years of the war, from 1939 to 1941, hiding in the Warsaw Ghetto with his mother and younger brother. In the early years of the war, his father, a physician and officer in the Polish Army, was captured by the Russians. Eventually, his mother was killed by the Nazis and Orlev and his brother were smuggled out of the ghetto and hidden by Polish families. In 1943, they were transported to the concentration camp Bergen-Belsen. In Bergen-Belsen, Orlev created stories to calm both himself and his brother, as everyone around them was killed. His stories helped to keep their spirit and will to survive alive.

After the war, Orlev immigrated to Israel where he studied and worked on a kibbutz. He left the kibbutz in 1962 and now lives in Jerusalem. He is married and has four children. Of his writing career, Orlev explains, "When I came to Israel after the war I learned a new language and lost the language of my childhood. And when I tried to write poetry I found that I was no longer able to. So I began to write stories, and later, books for adults." Orlev continued to write for adults until 1976, but since then, he has written more than 20 books for a younger audience and has received world-wide recognition both in Israel and around the world. *The Island on Bird Street* has been published in 10 languages.

SUMMARY

Loosely mirroring the author's own life experiences in the Warsaw ghetto, *The Island on Bird Street* is the gripping story of a young boy, Alex, who survives on his own in an empty ghetto—much like any ghetto established by the Nazis—sustained only by hope, the hope that his father would soon return to him.

In the final days of the ghetto's liquidation, Alex and his father are caught and marched to the trains for deportation. Alex manages to escape and hides in part of a house that was bombed at the beginning of the war. Using his ingenuity, he invents an incredible system for entering and leaving the house, while avoiding detection.

During his months alone, Alex is aided by several members of the Polish resistance who risk their own lives to save those of others and he, in turn, risks his life to save those of partisans who miraculously appear at his hideout at 78 Bird Street. Throughout the story, Alex must make life-and-death decisions as well as come to terms with the issues of right and wrong.

VOCABULARY **ghetto:** a designated area of a city to which Jews were restricted and from which they were forbidden to leave—ghetto inhabitants were forced to live with little food and under the most inhumane conditions.

larder: a place where the food supplies of a home are kept; pantry.

partisans: underground fighters who opposed Nazi occupation forces.

PREREADING ACTIVITY Read the book's introduction aloud to students. In it, the author compares the house in which the main character hides to a desert island, hence the title, *The Island on Bird Street.* Encourage students to list as many reasons as they can think of to substantiate this comparison by completing the phrase "The house is like a deserted island because..." When the book is completed, ask students to revisit their lists and make additions and deletions.

QUESTIONS AND ANSWERS

1. What is the significance of the book's title? (Alex hid in a house at 78 Bird Street. Throughout the book, he explains how life in the house is similar to life on a deserted island.)

2. To what did the term *retaliatory action* (page 6 of *The Island on Bird Street*) refer? (If a Jew lifted a hand against the Nazis, the Nazis would kill an additional number of men, women, and children to make certain it did not happen again.)

3. Who was Bolek and what part did he play in helping the Jews of the ghetto? (Bolek was part of the Polish underground. He was a political organizer, a Communist, who believed everyone was equal. He aided the partisans in their efforts against the Nazis.)

4. How did life in the ghetto serve to dehumanize people? (They lived in conditions that were subhuman. They lived without food, warmth, or adequate clothing. They lived surrounded by death, disease, and despair. Fear was their constant companion—fear of discovery and deportation. Survival was their only weapon.)

5. What characteristics did Alex possess that helped him survive? (smart, inventive, problem solver, imaginative, resourceful, etc.)

1. Alex realizes that it never occurred to the Nazis that a Jew might try to kill them. What might have been different if the Nazis had feared for their lives?

2. If the Nazis had not spent so much time, money, and manpower in their war against the Jews, how might the outcome of World War II have been affected—or would it have? Explain.

3. On the Polish side, next to the ghetto, Alex met many types of people, such as the doctor; the doorman at the entrance to the Polish side; Bolek; the woman informer; and Yanek, the bully. What similarities and differences do you see among these people? What makes them react so differently in a similar time and place? Describe a person you know who has something in common with one or more of these characters and explain.

4. Discuss the ways that Alex demonstrated the spirit of resistance. Cite specific examples from the book.

5. How does war change the way people live their lives? (Include emotional changes, their ideas of right and wrong, etc.)

1. After the war, several diaries were found in which the writers described life in the ghetto. Create a journal entry that might have been written by a person your age to describe one of the ghetto events you have read about in this book or in others as you researched ghetto life.

2. How do you explain the fact that there were so few people like the doctor and like Bolek, and so many more people like those Alex described as "rats"?

3. Alex was ashamed to admit that he had killed a German soldier. What advice would you give Alex about right and wrong and moral decisions such as the one Alex made?

4. Explain the role of the ghetto in the scheme of the "Final Solution" in the war against the Jews. What feelings did life in the ghetto evoke (i.e., feeling of isolation, etc.)?

5. Imagine that you have gone back in time and find yourself in one of the ghettos established by the Nazis. Write a journal entry to describe the sounds you hear within the ghetto, the sights you see. Describe your feelings as you witness these things. After writing this entry, share your insights with classmates in a group discussion.

EXTENSIONS

1. Through this story you have learned about Alex's struggle for survival. Find an article in the newspaper that describes the struggle for survival that other groups and/or individuals have endured. Share these articles by displaying them on a bulletin board. As a class, create an appropriate title for the board dealing with the struggle to survive.

2. Research various ghettos established by the Nazis in countries such as Poland and Germany. Create a classroom model of a ghetto to illustrate its main features. Discuss how a person could survive in this ghetto both spiritually and physically.

3. Research ghettos such as the one in Warsaw. In small groups, create a cluster or web of the word *ghetto*. Have each person create and present a monologue in which he/she expresses one specific aspect of life in the ghetto.

4. In the ghettos, the Nazis appointed a Jewish council to carry out their orders. Often, being part of this council, or Judenrat, created moral dilemmas. For example, at the end of the existence of the Warsaw Ghetto, each member of the Judenrat was ordered either to select a certain number of people a day for deportation or sacrifice his own family. As a class, discuss various dilemmas the Judenrat faced and list these. In groups, select one of these dilemmas and discuss the moral and ethical issues involved. Then describe the various options the Judenrat might have considered in dealing with the dilemma.

5. Resistance is the main theme of *The Island on Bird Street.* Use any form of media (artistic, musical, etc.) to express your feelings about the meaning of the word *resistance* as it pertains to the Holocaust.

Hannah Szenes: A Song of Light

Schur, Maxine. *Hannah Szenes: A Song of Light.* Philadelphia: The Jewish Publication Society, 1986.

ABOUT THE AUTHOR
Born in San Francisco, California, Maxine Schur's talents have led her to careers as a film editor, actress, an educational software designer, and an author. After completing her studies at the University of California at Berkeley, she and her husband traveled the world. For two years they explored more than 40 countries and traveled by almost every form of transportation imaginable—including donkey and tramp steamer.

In 1972, she made Wellington, New Zealand, her home and worked as an actress and film editor. Her travel experiences motivated her to write about her adventures, and these memories were sold to the New Zealand Department of Education to be made into a series of storybooks for children. Since that experience, writing has become a passion and she has authored numerous books.

Ms. Schur is back in the United States and lives in San Mateo, California.

SUMMARY
Hannah Szenes was in her early twenties when she left the relative safety of her new home in Israel to parachute into Yugoslavia to help free Jews there and in her native Hungary. Captured and branded a traitor, Szenes was tried and executed as a spy and traitor.

A Song of Light tells Hannah's story and gives us the opportunity to meet a remarkable young woman whose spirit and commitment to life led her to risk her own life to save others. The book includes many of the verses of poetry Hannah wrote and through her words we gain insight into a person who, from the age of six, was determined to "make a difference in the world...."

VOCABULARY
Zionism: the belief that Jews should return to Zion, their ancient homeland in Palestine, to create a nation once again.

kibbutz: a collective settlement.

Haganah: an underground military organization, founded in 1920, of the Yishuv, the Jewish community in Palestine.

PREREADING
ACTIVITY Ask each student to write his/her definition for the word *hero*. Divide students into groups and have them share their definitions and create one definition for the group. Discuss these definitions and list them on a chart. After reading the book *Hannah Szenes: A Song of Light*, have students determine how well Hannah Szenes fits their definitions of a hero/heroine.

QUESTIONS
AND
ANSWERS

1. When did Hannah first become aware of anti-Semitism? What happened to create this awareness? (Her tuition at Bar Maadas was three times the tuition of the non-Jewish students. When she questioned her mother about this policy she learned about the anti-Semitic propaganda coming out of Germany.)

2. What was the "stone that began the landslide" for Hungarian Jews, referred to on page 31? (The First Anti-Jewish Bill was passed in the Hungarian parliament. As a result, anti-Jewish actions became more acceptable.)

3. Why was Zionism so important to Hannah? (It renewed her pride in being Jewish; from the research she had done on the roots of anti-Semitism, she realized the importance of a Jewish homeland; it gave her, as she explained, "something to believe in...")

4. What was the White Paper? What was its effect on immigration to Palestine? (The White Paper of 1939 was a British piece of legislation that restricted Jewish emigration to Palestine. The White Paper limited the number of Jews allowed to enter Palestine. Of the millions that wished to emigrate, only 75,000 were given permission.)

5. Once she was living in Palestine, what made Hannah determined to return to Hungary? How did she achieve her goal? (She learned that the Third Anti-Jewish Bill had been passed in Hungary and that the new Prime Minister, Laszlo Bardossy, had sided with the Nazi attitude towards the Jewish people. Hitler ordered Bardossy to deport 800,000 Hungarian Jews, make the Jews wear the yellow Star of David armband, and take all money, land, and possessions belonging to the Jews. The Jews in Hungary now feared for their lives and Hannah wanted to help her mother escape, as well as help other Jews of Europe. She joined the Haganah, the Jewish Palestinian defense unit of the British Army, which sent soldiers to Europe to help the British soldiers and save as many Jewish citizens as possible.)

1. How did Hannah's decision to build S'dot Yam reflect her involvement in life in general?

2. What qualities did Hannah possess that caused her to be selected by the Haganah for its dangerous mission into Yugoslavia?

3. After being captured in Hungary, Hannah believed that she had failed in her mission. Do you agree or disagree with her assessment? Explain.

4. Why did the authorities in Hungary bother to put Hannah on trial when Jews throughout Europe were killed simply because they were Jewish?

5. Hannah made a vow to her father at his grave site. She promised to one day "make a difference in the world." Do you believe Hannah fulfilled this promise? Explain.

1. Hannah questioned who and what she really was. Based on your reading and knowledge of Hannah, write a letter to Hannah in answer to this soul-searching question.

2. What is the significance of the book's subtitle, *A Song of Light*? Read the poem on page 65 of the book and explain it in your own words.

3. Hannah explained that a certain line from the book *Broken Grindstones,* by the Hebrew novelist Hazaz, had a profound effect upon her. One line in the book says, "All the darkness can't extinguish a single candle, yet one candle can illuminate all the darkness." Interpret this quote and describe what it says to you. Can you give an example of a person you know who has illuminated the darkness with a special deed or action?

4. Why is the name Hannah Szenes now legend? What does it represent and stand for?

5. Read the poem on the final page of the book. Write a journal entry that describes how people who have died can continue to light the world.

EXTENSIONS

1. Create a poem in tribute to Hannah Szenes the poet and/or Hannah Szenes the rescuer. Use your poem to express your feelings about Hannah and her life. As an alternative, you may wish to select your favorite poem from those written by Hannah Szenes. Read it aloud to the class and discuss its significance to you.

2. Locate Hungary on a world map. What countries border it? Create a time frame of the events in Hungary leading up to the final extermination of its Jewish citizens. Compare these events with events in other countries bordering Hungary. What similarities and differences can you find?

3. Read other books about Hannah Szenes such as *In Kindling Flame*: *The Story of Hannah Senesh 1921–1944,* by Linda Atkinson (Lothrop). Which book most helped you understand Hannah, her life, and her motivation for becoming a rescuer? Which would you recommend to others your age? Why? Prepare and present a book talk (brief summary of the book that is given to inspire others to read it) to your classmates.

4. Hannah dreamed of one day traveling from kibbutz to kibbutz telling the stories of the paratroopers and what happened. Help fulfill this dream by traveling from classroom to classroom telling the story of Hannah and her friends who parachuted into Yugoslavia to save the lives of countless others.

5. Select several favorite quotes from Hannah's journals and poems. Illustrate each and combine them with those selected by your classmates to create a book dedicated to Hannah and her ideals. From the various quotes, choose the one that is most special to you and in a class discussion explain your choice.

The Short Life of Sophie Scholl

Vinke, Hermann. *The Short Life of Sophie Scholl.* New York: Harper and Row, 1980.

ABOUT THE AUTHOR

If you would like information about the author, Hermann Vinke, write to him care of the publisher, HarperCollins, 10 East 53rd Street, New York, NY 10022. On the envelope, write the words "author mail." Your letters will be forwarded.

SUMMARY

The Short Life of Sophie Scholl introduces us to Sophie through her own letters, diary entries, and through the memories of family, friends, and others whose lives she touched.

At a young age, Sophie Scholl knew that the Nazi regime was synonymous with evil. Her early upbringing taught her to think independently, to express her beliefs despite the perceptions of others, and to act upon those beliefs. And she knew that one person could make a difference.

With a small group of other non-Jewish teens and young adults, Sophie joined the White Rose, an underground organization of students who dedicated themselves to creating an understanding in fellow Germans of the immorality of the Nazi regime. Through leaflets that they wrote, published, and distributed, the White Rose was successful in heightening awareness and encouraging others to work together to resist the Nazis. Sophie and her brother knew that their work put their lives in danger, but their dedication to the ideals of freedom and free thought preempted all else.

The Nazis, concerned about the leaflets that were finding their way into hands across the land, brought the members of White Rose to trial for treason. Sophie Scholl and her brother Hans, both at the heart of the White Rose, were found guilty and sentenced to death. They were executed on February 22, 1943, two months before Sophie's twenty-second birthday. They faced their deaths with courage and with the conviction that what they had accomplished would cause others to further resist the Nazis and bring freedom to their land and their people.

VOCABULARY

The White Rose: an underground youth movement dedicated to calling attention to the immorality of the Nazi regime.

Gestapo: the Secret State Police.

Hitlerjugend (HJ): the Hitler Youth, a political organization that, through propaganda and other devices, polarized the youth of Germany to follow, without question, the dictates of the Nazi government. Various divisions of the Hitler Youth existed and membership was determined by age and gender.

Deutsche Jungenschaft vom 1. November (German Boys' League of the First of November or d.j.1.11): An offspring of the youth leagues, this movement rediscovered nature, the environment, and literature. Free thought was encouraged.

PREREADING ACTIVITY Introduce Sophie Scholl to the class with the following quote taken from one of her journal entries: "You must have a hard spirit and a soft heart." Discuss what this phrase means and what type of person Sophie might be. After reading the book or excerpts of it, ask students to again interpret the quote in terms of what they now know about Sophie Scholl and her life.

QUESTIONS AND ANSWERS

1. Describe Sophie's early life. (Born into a closely knit middle-class family, Sophie's home was filled with books, music, and love. Literature and politics were openly discussed and she and her brothers and sisters were encouraged to be critical thinkers and to form their own conclusions. Her father was known for his liberal and progressive ideas.)

2. How did Sophie demonstrate her unwillingness just to go along with the crowd? (While there are many such examples, they include these: anytime she saw someone treated unfairly, Sophie fought back and voiced her protest; she could not accept anti-Jewish racism and maintained her friendship with a Jewish friend; and she recommended the reading of Heinrich Heine, whose work was banned because he was Jewish.)

3. Why did Sophie join the Hitler Youth Movement? What did it represent to her? What changed her attitude? (Sophie joined the movement as did most of her friends and siblings. At first, Sophie believed the Hitler movement's promises of greatness, happiness, and prosperity. As time went on, Sophie was outraged at the things the regime did to keep their promises. As she listened to their politics and philosophy, as she witnessed the way in which freedoms were being taken from individuals and groups, she became more and more disenchanted.)

4. What was the White Rose? Why did Sophie and Hans join this group? (The White Rose was an underground movement formed to protest the Nazi regime. Its members were generally young German non-Jewish youths in their late teens and early twenties. Both Sophie and Hans became leaders of the White Rose and were dedicated to creating an awareness in their fellow German citizens concerning the immoral nature of the Nazi movement. They hoped to encourage others to protest and resist the Nazis and all for which they stood.)

5. Fritz Hartnagel, Sophie's friend, explained that it was Sophie who finally persuaded him to admit that Germany had to lose the war. He said that he had also seen many things, especially dealing with the persecution of Jews, that further supported this admission. Describe what Hartnagel had witnessed. (businesses being taken away from their Jewish owners; the disappearance of Jewish people; friends being taken to concentration camps; organized assaults on Jews, Jewish businesses, and synagogues)

DISCUSSION TOPICS

1. Discuss the importance of literature in Sophie's life. What impact did it have upon her and her values?

2. How did Sophie help bring out the best in others? Cite specific instances from the book.

3. What is meant by passive resistance? Describe instances of passive resistance and explain how the White Rose was a successful example of such a resistance movement.

4. What factors in a person's life and/or background might cause him/her to say "no" to racism and murder while others simply turn their heads?

5. Discuss the importance of independent/critical thinking. How does this ability affect your life? How can critical thinking skills in students your age be improved?

WRITING TOPICS

1. Create a portrait of Sophie with words alone in such a way that readers will know her inside and outside.

2. A line from a Goëthe poem was often quoted by Sophie's father and was of special significance to Sophie. Explain what the line, "Braving all powers, Holding your own" meant to Sophie? What do these words say to you?

3. Reread the portions of the pamphlets the White Rose distributed that were included in the book. Select a favorite portion and paraphrase it.

4. Write a journal entry as if you were Sophie, explaining whether or not you would make the same choice—choosing resistance—if given the opportunity again.

5. What can today's youth learn from reading *The Short Life of Sophie Scholl?*

EXTENSIONS

1. What one quote do you think best summarizes Sophie's reasons for resistance? Copy it, illustrate it, share it with your classmates, and then combine it with those selected by other students to create a book dedicated to Sophie and the members of the White Rose. As a class, create a forward to this book and give it a special title worthy of the subject.

2. Imagine you are Sophie's attorney during the trial in which she and her brother were accused of high treason. Prepare a speech (or closing argument) in which you defend the actions of Sophie Scholl and the members of the White Rose. Deliver this speech to your class.

3. On a class mural, respond to the phrase "Resistance is..." with either words or pictures. As you continue reading about Sophie Scholl and learning more about the Holocaust, continue adding to this mural.

4. Read the picture book *Rose Blanche* by Roberto Innocenti (Stewart, Tabori and Chang, New York, 1991). This is the story of a young girl who discovers a concentration camp with hungry, cold children and is moved to make secret journeys to bring food to these small victims. The title character of the book was named for the White Rose. Lead a discussion of the book and the way certain individuals, in their own ways, resisted the Nazis.

5. With a small group of students, plan and prepare a short leaflet that will inspire others to fight against a wrong facing our lives today. As you create this, think, "What would Sophie do?" Share this leaflet with other students and discuss your ideas.

Daniel's Story

Matas, Carol. *Daniel's Story.* New York: Scholastic, 1993.

ABOUT THE AUTHOR

Carol Matas lives in Winnipeg, Canada, with her husband and two children. She attended the University of Western Ontario where she received her degree in English Literature. Ms. Matas did not originally plan a career in writing. Instead, she had trained to be an actor in Toronto, Canada. It was the fantasy story of a friend that inspired her to write her first piece of fiction. She continued to write, more as a hobby than anything else, but events in her life conspired to encourage her writing. Now a full-time writer, Ms. Matas has written many popular books for children, including *Sworn Enemies, The D. N. A. Dimensions,* and *The Fusion Factor.* In 1993, *Sworn Enemies* was the recipient of the Sydney Taylor Book Award, which honors outstanding contributions to the field of Jewish literature for children.

In March 1992, Ms. Matas was called by her agent and asked if she would write a book, a companion piece to the exhibit "Daniel's Story: Remember the Children," being created for the U.S. Holocaust Memorial Museum. The book, she points out, is not a novelization of the exhibit. Instead, it is a work of historical fiction, and Daniel is a composite of millions of children who were victims of the Holocaust. The book was quite a challenge for a number of reasons. The "ultimate difficulty," she says, was facing the subject matter, "the worst of the human spirit." But face the challenge she did, and *Daniel's Story* is touching readers in a way few books have ever been able to do.

SUMMARY

Although Daniel is a fictitious character, the events depicted in the story are real. *Daniel's Story* is a compilation of the experiences of over one million children who died in the Holocaust. The book was published in conjunction with an exhibit at the United States Holocaust Memorial Museum in Washington, D. C., called "Daniel's Story: Remember the Children." Daniel's story begins in Frankfurt, Germany, and the events of his life unfold as he leafs through the pictures of his photograph album and recounts the memories they inspire. From Frankfurt he and his family are relocated to the Lodz ghetto in Poland. From there, Daniel is transported to the Auschwitz Concentration Camp and finally to the concentration camp at Buchenwald. His journey is one accompanied by hope and courage as he struggles to survive in a world of death and despair.

VOCABULARY   **Black Shirts:** the German police (SS), organized in 1925 and later developed into the units that operated the concentration camps.

Brown Shirts: the storm troopers (SA), organized in 1920 by the Nazi Party to intimidate the opposition.

displaced person camps: administered by the Allies at the end of the war, these camps gave survivors a place to stay as they tried to put their lives back together.

ghetto: an enclosed area of a city in which the Jews were forced to live.

kapo: prisoner (often a criminal) in charge of one of the barracks in the concentration camps.

Kristallnacht: the Night of Broken Glass, November 9-10, 1938, in which synagogues across Germany were burned, and Jewish businesses, homes, and schools were vandalized.

PREREADING ACTIVITY   Based on their knowledge of the Holocaust, encourage students to discuss the pictures on the front cover of the book. What is happening in each? What might the people in the pictures be thinking? What do they see?

QUESTIONS AND ANSWERS

1. Why did Daniel's family, like so many others, find it difficult to imagine that the Jews would be sent out of Germany? (Jewish people had lived in relative peace in Germany for generations.)

2. When they finally realized that they had to leave Germany, why were Daniel and his family unable to do so? (They were unable to get visas from any countries. Even the United States, with a quota not yet filled from people in Germany, would not allow any more Jewish immigrants.)

3. What were the Nuremberg Laws? Why were they designed? (They were laws that took away citizenship from Jews along with many of their rights, such as the right to vote and the right to marry whomever they choose [Jewish people were forbidden to marry non-Jews]. These laws were passed to protect German "purity.")

4. What was Kristallnacht? Why was it such a significant event? (Literally, it means "the night of broken glass." It marked the beginning of overt terrorism against the Jewish people.)

5. Why was Daniel's friend killed in Poland after the war had ended? (It made no difference to the people whether or not the war was over—they still wanted to make certain that no Jewish people survived. This type of killing occurred in villages throughout Poland.)

DISCUSSION TOPICS

1. Discuss the test the Nazis devised to measure intelligence and the irony behind their conclusions.

2. Locate the main concentration camps established by the Germans (use the map in *Daniel's Story* as well as other references). Why do you think these locations were selected?

3. Why was the Hitler Youth Movement so appealing to German youths?

4. Why did membership in the Hitler Youth Movement seem to allow its participants to forget any moral standards, as Daniel suggests? Give examples of how similar membership (i.e., gangs) has a similar effect.

5. In many ways, Daniel was a resistance fighter. Cite examples from this book to support this statement.

WRITING TOPICS

1. Daniel kept a photo album that represented important people and times in his life. Imagine that, instead, Daniel kept a journal. As Daniel, write a journal entry that describes one of the important people or events in his life.

2. Write a one-line message to Daniel that reflects your feelings about his story. Share this with your classmates and display it on a bulletin board entitled "A Note to Daniel."

3. What was your first reaction to learning that the United States would not fill its entry quota with people fleeing Nazi Germany?

4. At the end of the book, Daniel asks Rosa how they will have the strength to continue. Reread Rosa's response. How would you respond to this question?

5. Could events similar to those that led to the Holocaust occur today in the United States? Could rights, for example, be taken away from a specific group of people, and could public attitude towards a single group be completely altered? Explain your answer.

EXTENSIONS

1. Recreate Daniel's album by drawing your own pictures and by finding appropriate photographs in magazines and books about the Holocaust that correlate with the descriptions he gave of his life. Divide the album into the following categories: Pictures of Frankfurt; Pictures of Lodz; Pictures of Auschwitz; Pictures of Buchenwald. Each group of students should be responsible for the pictures in one of these categories and for adding captions to the pictures.

2. Create a time line of events in Daniel's life to get a picture of the Holocaust years. The time line can be a class project, each student placing one event on a time line that stretches across the classroom.

3. In the book, Rosa and Erika debate what is needed to survive. Erika believes that if they can hold out long enough, the war will end before they are killed. She believes hope is their only resource. Rosa, on the other hand, believes that hope is the enemy. She believes hope should be replaced by guns and fighting back. With others in your class, debate this issue. Use your knowledge of the times to help you.

4. Create a class collage using words and pictures to depict impressions you and your classmates have of the Holocaust and the nightmare Daniel and his family were forced to endure.

5. Any mention of the Holocaust is accompanied by the word "Remember." Since poetry expresses our deepest emotions, create a poem that either captures a specific remembrance of the Holocaust or that expresses the importance of remembering.

Remember

Yesterday's nightmare
The darkness of blind hatred
Worlds torn and shattered
Yet tomorrow's legacy
But for our remembering

The Devil's Arithmetic

Yolen, Jane. *The Devil's Arithmetic.* New York: Viking, 1988.

ABOUT THE AUTHOR

A multi-talented author, folk singer, critic, and editor, Jane Yolen was born in New York City on February 11, 1939. She comes from a family of writers and storytellers—her father has written books and radio scripts and her mother has written short stories and crossword puzzles. Originally, Yolen had planned to be a journalist but discovered she was too emotional to do interviews. During college she continually worked to develop her writing talents, and many of the stories and poetry she wrote at that time were published in magazines and newspapers. In addition to authoring an incredible number of award-winning books, including the Caldecott Award Winner *Owl Moon,* Yolen's enthusiasm for life has led her to climb a mountain in Greece, work on an orange grove in Israel, drive a dogsled in Alaska, and raft down the Colorado River.

Yolen considers herself a poet and a storyteller. Her writing takes us on voyages of discovery and allows us to explore the joys and sadnesses of life.

SUMMARY

Thirteen-year-old Hannah is tired of remembering. At the traditional Passover Seder she resents having to listen to stories of the past and is tired of her grandfather's anger to any reference to the Holocaust. But, as Hannah opens the door to symbolically welcome Elijah, the Prophet, she suddenly finds that she has walked into the past. She finds herself in a small village in Poland with only her memories of the present. Gradually, Hannah forgets what "is" and becomes Chaya, and she and her family are ultimately transported by the Nazis to a death camp.

Though it has elements of fantasy, *The Devil's Arithmetic* describes the stark reality of life and death in the concentration camps.

VOCABULARY

Passover: a Jewish holiday observed in remembrance of the Jewish exodus from Egypt when the Jews were slaves.

Seder: the traditional dinner held on the first evening of Passover. The word *seder* literally means "order."

Haggadah: guidebook used during the Seder which explains the significance of Passover, retells the story of the exodus, and includes prayers and songs.

shtetl: a small Jewish village.

Note: Throughout the book, many Yiddish words are printed in italics. Encourage students to use context clues to determine the meanings for these words.

PREREADING ACTIVITY Have students come up with their own definitions for the title words *The Devil's Arithmetic.* Have them put their definitions on strips of posterboard and illustrate. Allow time for them to discuss their definitions. After completing the book, discuss the definitions again to see which came closest to the book's interpretation.

QUESTIONS AND ANSWERS

1. Compare Hannah's life in New Rochelle with Chaya's life in the shtetl. (Life in the two cultures was completely different. For example, in the shtetl, girls did not go to school, villagers did not mingle much with people of other religions, they never went to movies, spouses were selected by parents.)

2. List some of the euphemisms (words or phrases substituted for another) used during the Holocaust and explain why so many of them became part of the language of the concentration camps. (By using euphemisms the Nazis felt they could not be blamed for what had happened. If they never used the words *crematorium* or *gas chamber,* then they believed there was no proof that they existed—what is not recorded cannot be blamed. Some euphemisms included the following: "chosen" meant selected for death; "processed" referred to cremated; "showers" referred to the gas chambers.)

3. Why did the Nazis tattoo numbers on the arms of the prisoners in the Auschwitz concentration camp? (It helped to dehumanize them by taking away their identity, and it simplified the Nazi method of recordkeeping.)

4. How did the prisoners use the tattooed numbers to their benefit? (They associated each number of the tattoo with something relevant to their own lives and this, in turn, helped them identify themselves as human beings. For example, Rivka explained the significance of each number and letter on her arm to Chaya—the "J" was for Jewish, the "1" because she was alone, and so on. By recognizing each person's number at a glance, the prisoners could decode the Nazis' records and know their plans for the various prisoners.)

5. Why did Rivka and Wolf change their names? (To help them forget their past—although they never could—remembering was too painful.)

DISCUSSION TOPICS

1. At the beginning of the book, Hannah is tired of remembering. By the end of her experience, what had she learned about the importance of the word *remember*?

2. In the final pages of the book, Jane Yolen quotes Emmanuel Ringelblum, a Jewish historian of the Holocaust, concerning his definition of the heroism of the common Jew. Do you agree or disagree with Ringelblum's evaluation? Explain your answer.

3. Over the entrance of Auschwitz Concentration Camp are the words *Arbeit Macht Frei*, which translates to "Work Makes You Free." Discuss the irony of these words.

4. In every book dealing with the Holocaust, there are explanations for how the Germans were able to so efficiently kill so many millions of people. What factors do you believe were the most significant in contributing to their ability to destroy?

5. What additional insights did you gain concerning the Holocaust as a result of reading *The Devil's Arithmetic*?

WRITING TOPICS

1. During the wedding procession to Viosk, Hannah/Chaya meets the *badchan*, who, as a type of jester, speaks many truths in jest. Select one of the quotes of the *badchan* and explain the wisdom behind the words.

2. Study the illustrations on the front and back covers of the book. Select one of the pictures and describe it and its significance, based on insights you have gained from the book and from your study of the Holocaust. In your description, use words that will stimulate the senses and allow the reader to gain a deeper meaning.

3. Describe how the concentration camps give new meaning to the words *cruelty* and *inhumanity*.

4. How would you define the word *hope*? What part does hope play in survival?

5. Many people have their own definitions of the word *hero*. What is your definition of the word? Which character in *The Devil's Arithmetic* most meets your definition? Cite specific references from the book to support your answer.

EXTENSIONS   1. Create a word cluster for the word *prejudice.* Create a word cluster for the word *acceptance.* Create a contrast poem that expresses your feelings toward these two words.

Example:

PREJUDICE
vicious cruel
uncompromising debilitating destroying
evil sickness peace life
understanding cooperating caring
bright hopeful
ACCEPTANCE

2. Select one of the events described in *The Devil's Arithmetic* and create a picture to accompany the text.

3. Assume you are a friend of Chaya's who was with her during the time she was in Auschwitz. Write a letter to Chaya expressing your own hopes and fears while trying to stay alive.

4. Using any artistic, dramatic, or written form, explain *The Devil's Arithmetic.* Compile these into a class book.

5. In the final pages of the book, Jane Yolen quotes Winston Churchill who wrote, "There is no doubt that this is probably the greatest and most horrible single crime ever committed in the history of the world." In fact, there is more proof, more documentation of the Holocaust than of any other happening in the history of humankind. Obtain a video of a survivor's testimony by requesting a copy from one of the Holocaust Documentation Centers (see Resources). With others in the class, discuss your reactions and reflections after watching this documented video.

Alicia: My Story

Appleman-Jurman, Alicia. *Alicia: My Story.* New York: Bantam Books, 1988.

ABOUT THE AUTHOR

Alicia Appleman-Jurman was a young Jewish girl living in East Poland when Germany signed a peace treaty with Russia, and Hitler and Stalin divided Poland between them. Through the Holocaust years, her brothers and father were killed, leaving Alicia and her mother alone to survive the terrors and horrors of Nazi occupation.

During the war years, Alicia survived through her courage and innate abilities. She spoke several languages fluently, and worked the fields for both the Polish and Ukrainian farmers, in exchange for bread. Despite the incredible hardships and pain she had to endure, Alicia saved the lives of many others as she fled through war-ravaged Poland.

After the war, Alicia continued to put the needs of others before her own. She led groups of Jewish people through underground routes to freedom in what is now Israel. After becoming quite ill, Alicia was finally sent to Palestine. Immediately upon reaching Israel, however, she was transferred to a military prison on the island of Cyprus, where she remained for eight months. When she was finally released, Alicia moved to Haifa, where she met and later married an American volunteer who worked as an engineer.

In 1952, Alicia moved to America. She now lives in California with her husband and is the mother of three grown children. Over the years, Alicia has devoted her time to telling her story in the hope that today's youth will learn from the past so that "evil forces will never again be permitted to set one people against another."

SUMMARY

Alicia: My Story is the autobiography of a remarkable girl who survived against the most unbelievable odds. Her story is one of real people in a world gone mad. Through her eyes we discover both extremes of human expression—cruelty and kindness; and through her words we learn of destruction and death and of hope and courage.

Through Alicia's account, we too become witnesses to the events of the Holocaust. Alicia takes us from a small village in East Poland to Nazi prisons and remote farmhouses; she takes us from underground bunkers to the edges of burning pits; she takes us from one nightmare to the next.

Alicia's story is the story of unequaled heroism. Though only to the tiniest degree, we begin to recognize the incredible determination and strength of character upon which survival depends. *Alicia: My Story* becomes the story of all those who prevailed against overwhelming odds and reminds us of individual responsibility in ensuring "Never again."

VOCABULARY

Judenrat: committee who represented the Jewish community to the German authorities.

partisans: underground fighters against Nazi occupation forces, they mainly fought in the forests in White Russia, Poland, and Lithuania.

Zionism: a movement formerly for reestablishing, now for advancing, the Jewish homeland in Israel.

aliyah: immigrations of Jews to Israel.

pogroms: random and unprovoked attacks against Jewish villages begun by the Russian Cossacks.

PREREADING ACTIVITY

Read the comments and reviews that appear on the back cover. Have students discuss their predictions concerning Alicia and her life based on the reviews alone. Record their predictions and, after completing the book, compare the reality with what they imagined.

QUESTIONS AND ANSWERS

1. What was life like for Alicia and her family before the Holocaust? (They were a close family, well-respected in the community by Jews and non-Jews alike. Education was a priority and the family lived comfortably.)

2. Since it did not have a wall around it, how were people forced to remain in the ghetto into which Alicia's family moved? (Leaving the ghetto was punishable by death. Few wanted to risk this repercussion.)

3. What languages did Alicia speak and how did her ability to speak so many languages aid her in surviving? (She spoke Russian, Polish, Ukrainian, and Hebrew. Her fluency in these languages helped her as she lived in the forests and the fields, trying to find work in exchange for food. Her knowledge of languages helped her determine who were friends and who were enemies; it

enabled her to discover what dangers were ahead as she overheard different conversations; and her ability allowed her to help other survivors immigrate to Israel.)

4. Why was Palestine governed by the British in the 1940s? (It was mandated by the old League of Nations.)

5. Why was it necessary for so many to reach Israel illegally rather than through the legal channels? (Britain's foreign secretary, Bevin, issued a "White Paper" that limited the entry of Jews into Palestine. England wanted to pacify the Arab nations which opposed a Jewish homeland, despite the fact that such a place was promised in the Balfour Declaration of 1917.)

DISCUSSION TOPICS

1. Who were the people who helped Alicia survive? What were the motives of each? Of these people, whom do you admire most? Explain.

2. What one factor was most responsible for Alicia's survival—her love of family or her hate of the enemy? Cite specific references in the book to support your opinion.

3. Of all the things that Alicia had to overcome, what do you think took the most courage? Explain.

4. Why did so many people close their minds and hearts to what was happening to their Jewish neighbors? To what extent was this dictated by personal fears and/or by self-interest?

5. Alicia explained that many who survived the Holocaust felt guilty. How would you explain this phenomenon?

WRITING TOPICS

1. In your journal, respond to the following question: "If you were placed in the same circumstances and time as Alicia, do you believe you would have survived? Why or why not?"

2. Alicia wrote that the only way to fight evil is with good. Describe what you can do in your own life to ensure that good triumphs over evil.

3. One of the most important words in the Hebrew language is *shalom*—peace. People use this word as they greet one another and when they are saying good-bye. Explain the significance of this word to *all* people.

4. Imagine that you are Alicia. What questions or things would you like to ask your neighbors and friends who did little to help you and your family?

5. The forest protected Alicia in many ways and was her home for many months. Metaphorically, Alicia's life could be compared to a forest. Explain.

EXTENSIONS

1. Individually or in small groups, respond to the following:

   I used to think _____,

   but now I know _____.

   In response to the first line, write impressions/ideas you had before reading the book. In response to the second line, write new impressions/ideas formed after reading *Alicia: My Story*. Repeat this process to create several verses.

   > Example: I used to think that only those in concentration camps were victims of the Holocaust.

   > But now I know that victims of the Holocaust were everywhere—in the ghettos, in the fields, in the forests....

2. Select a song whose lyrics mirror feelings you have after reading *Alicia: My Story* (i.e., "Imagine," by John Lennon). Distribute a copy of the words to your classmates and then explain the ways the song reflects ideas, attitudes, and feelings stimulated by the book.

3. After most of the Jewish population had been killed, the Ukrainians turned their guns on the Poles. Alicia wrote, "When you heap suffering on others, some of it can't help but fall back on you." Create a poster that expresses this understanding in your own words. Illustrate it and display it in your classroom.

4. Alicia joined the organization PaChaCh which was concerned with sharing news of the world and with saving all people. With your classmates, create an organization that is dedicated to learning about injustices against people and works to call public attention to what needs to be done to right these wrongs.

5. Watch the movie *Exodus*. (Available at most video rental stores.) Discuss how the movie reinforced many of the things Alicia wrote about concerning legal and illegal immigration to Israel.

Anne Frank: The Diary of a Young Girl

Frank, Anne. *Anne Frank: The Diary of a Young Girl.*
  New York: Doubleday, 1967.

Anne Frank: Beyond the Diary

Van der Rol, Ruud and Verhoeven, Rian. *Anne
Frank: Beyond the Diary.* New York: Viking, 1993.

Note: Although either book can be used without the other, the books work well together to give students an increased understanding of Anne Frank and her world. The majority of questions and activities in this unit relate to *Anne Frank: The Diary of a Young Girl.* Those that also rely on *Anne Frank: Beyond the Diary* are preceded by an asterisk (*).

ABOUT THE AUTHOR

Anne Frank: The Diary of a Young Girl

Anne Frank was born in Frankfurt-am-Main, Germany, in 1929, the daughter of Edith and Otto Frank. Her early childhood was a happy one, shared with a loving family which included her older sister Margot. By 1933, as the campaign of death and destruction aimed at the Jewish people became more evident, Anne and her family moved to Amsterdam, where her father had the opportunity to begin a new business.

Anne was given a diary for her thirteenth birthday—June 12, 1942. Less than one month later, she and her family were forced into hiding when the Nazis, in their goal to annihilate all the Jews of Europe, called Margot for deportation. Life in hiding was difficult, but Anne's spirit and courage allowed her to soar beyond the physical restraints. In her diary, Anne shared her innermost thoughts and dreams and recorded her observations and reflections about life in the secret annex. After two years in hiding, Anne and her family were discovered and deported to concentration camps. Eventually, she and her sister were transferred to Bergen-Belsen. Due to the incredibly inhumane conditions and treatment, both girls contracted typhus. Margot died in March 1945, and a few days later, Anne died—only weeks before the British liberated the camp. She was 15 years old.

Anne Frank: Beyond the Diary

Ruud van der Rol is a sociologist and Rian Verhoeven is a historian. Both are on the staff of the Anne Frank House in Amsterdam, a museum and foundation dedicated to promoting Anne's ideals. Van der Rol and Verhoeven work in the Educational Department where they assist with the *Anne Frank Journal,* an annual publication. In addition, both present student programs addressing topics concerning World War II, racism, and discrimination.

Anne Frank: The Diary of a Young Girl

Through the pages of Anne Frank's diary, we are given a glimpse of a life in hiding. Anne confided in her diary as a person would to a best friend. The pages of the diary reveal the events of World War II and the Holocaust, as witnessed by one of its victims, and is also a deeply revealing commentary on human nature. The first entry of the diary was dated June 14, 1942, two days after Anne's thirteenth birthday, and the last entry was written Tuesday, August 1, 1944, just days before the Gestapo invaded the hiding place and deported Anne, her family, and the four others who shared their secret place.

Anne Frank: Beyond the Diary

This photographic remembrance of the life of Anne Frank includes historical essays and photographs along with excerpts from the diary to provide us with increased understanding of Anne and her family. The book fills in many of the gaps by including information from events preceding and following those included in *The Diary of a Young Girl*. The photographs were provided from those compiled by the Anne Frank House and those provided by Elfriede Frank, Otto Frank's widow, and Miep Gies, the woman who risked her life to help Anne and her family hide in the secret annex.

VOCABULARY   **annex(e):** an addition to a building

typhus: an acute infectious disease caused by a rickettsia transmitted to humans by the bite of fleas, lice, etc. Typhus is characterized by fever, nervous disorders, and weakness and often results in death.

PREREADING ACTIVITY   Discuss the purpose of keeping a diary. Involve students in a discussion of the following: What type of information is usually included in a diary? How is a diary a person's individual history? How does a diary reflect the times?

QUESTIONS AND ANSWERS

1. Why did Anne begin her diary entries with "Dear Kitty"? (She wanted a close friend in whom she could confide. The diary was to be this close friend.)

2. When and where was Anne Frank born? How old was she when she began her diary? (Anne was born in Frankfurt-am-Main, Germany, on June 12, 1929. She began her diary when she was 13.)

3. What anti-Jewish decrees did Anne describe in her diary entry of June 20, 1942? (Jews had to wear a yellow star, they had to hand in their bicycles, they

were banned from trams and forbidden to drive. They were allowed to do their shopping only within certain hours and only in places labeled "Jewish shop." They were given a curfew and had to be inside after 8 o'clock in the evening. They were forbidden from visiting theaters, cinemas, and other places of entertainment. They were not allowed to take part in public sports nor were they allowed to visit any public sports grounds. They were not allowed to visit Christians and were required to attend only Jewish schools.)

4. What events caused the Frank family to go into hiding? (The Nazis in Amsterdam began rounding up Jewish people for deportation to the death camps. On July 5, 1942, Margot was summoned for deportation.)

5. How were the Franks and the others hiding in the secret annex able to survive there for such a long period of time—how did they get food and other necessities? (They were aided by non-Jewish friends who detested the Nazi occupation and treatment of the Jewish people.)

*6. In *The Diary of a Young Girl,* Anne renamed the people who shared the secret annex as well as those who helped hide them. *Beyond the Diary* explains who these people really were. List the true identities of the people in the secret annex and the names of the friends who tried to save them. (Mr. Koophuis— Johannes Kleiman; Mr. Kraler—Victor Kugler; Elli Vossen—Bep Voskuijl; Mr. Vossen—Mr. Voskuijl; Miep van Santen—Miep Gies; Henk van Santen—Jan Gies; The Van Daan family—the Van Pels family; Albert Dussel—Fritz Pfeffer.)

DISCUSSION TOPICS

1. What do you and your friends have in common with Anne?

2. In the introduction to the book, Eleanor Roosevelt said that Anne's diary shows the "nobility of the spirit." Cite examples from Anne's diary that exemplify this.

3. What were some of the most difficult aspects of a life in hiding?

4. What insights have you gained from Anne's diary about World War II and the Holocaust?

5. Anne Frank's wish to "go on living even after [her] death" has come true. How will you remember Anne?

*6. Study the pictures of Anne and her family in *Beyond the Diary;* how would you describe the Frank family and their life before they left Germany?

*7. Study the map on pages 94–95 in *Beyond the Diary,* as well as the statistics given. What inferences can you make based solely on the information on these two pages?

WRITING TOPICS

1. Close your eyes and imagine that you are looking through Anne's window in the attic of the secret annex. Describe what you see, hear, and feel.

2. After reading Anne's diary, reread the introduction written by Eleanor Roosevelt. Write your own introduction to the diary to express your reactions and impressions.

3. The Anne Frank House in Amsterdam is now a museum and foundation committed to promoting Anne's ideals. What are these ideals? If Anne were alive today, what would she want people your age to understand? Write a one-page entry that might have been Anne's message to the youth of today.

4. Create a biographical sketch of Anne. Use quotes from Anne that especially help to illustrate the type of person she was.

5. Of all the characters described in the diary, which do you find most "heroic"? Explain your answer and then hold a class discussion in which each student defends his/her choice.

*6. Select one photograph from *Beyond the Diary* that affects you in some way. In your journal, describe the picture and your reactions to it. Share your entry with the rest of the class.

*7. Compare your description in writing activity #1 above after looking at actual pictures of the view from the secret annex. How do the photographs change your perceptions?

EXTENSIONS

1. *The Diary of a Young Girl* has, as the book's afterword explains, achieved enormous popularity. It has been published in 30 countries and sold more than one million copies in hardcover alone. Imagine that you are a book review critic for your local newspaper. Write an article that describes this incredible work and explains the phenomena described by Ernst Schnabel, the author of *Anne Frank: A Portrait in Courage,* "Her voice was preserved out of the millions that were silenced, this voice no louder than a child's whisper...It has outlasted the shouts of the murderers and has soared above the voices of time."

2. The original Dutch title for *The Diary of a Young Girl* was *Het Achterhuis,* which refers to the hiding place. *Achter* means "behind" or "in back of" and *huis* is Dutch for "house." Read another book about victims of the Nazis who tried to escape through hiding in attics, closets, bunkers, etc., such as *The Upstairs Room* by Johanna Reiss (HarperCollins, 1990). Compare the experiences of these people who were in hiding with those expressed by Anne.

3. Read *Anne Frank's Tales From the Secret Annex* (Doubleday, 1984) a collection of short stories, essays, and fables written by Anne while she was in hiding. Select a favorite tale and share it with your classmates.

4. Movies and videos have been created based on the life of Anne Frank (see Resources). With your classmates, watch one of these. Discuss whether or not the movie/video extended the feelings and understandings generated from Anne's diary.

5. Begin a diary of your own. Include your reflections on the happenings and events that impact your life.

*6. *Beyond the Diary* includes pieces of Anne's life from before her diary was begun and from after it ended. Select one aspect of Anne's life from a time not included in the diary. Create a diary entry (with date) and write it as Anne might have.

*7. Frequently we take our lives and freedoms for granted. To better understand the way in which Anne lived for almost two years, recreate a model of the secret annex based on the drawings and diagrams included in *Beyond the Diary.* Place this model on display in the classroom along with a key that explains/labels the various areas.

Night

Wiesel, Elie. *Night.* New York: Bantam Books, 1986. (Original copyright 1960).

ABOUT THE AUTHOR

Elie Wiesel was only twelve years old when, in 1941, the events of World War II and the Holocaust invaded his home in Sighet, Transylvania. His childhood was cut short, his dreams and beliefs shattered, as he witnessed the death of his family and his people in the Nazi death camps of Auschwitz and Buchenwald. After the war, Wiesel took a 10-year vow of silence before he attempted to put into words the horror and pain of the Holocaust. When he finally wrote *Night*, Wiesel had difficulty finding a publisher, for it was believed that few would want to read such heart-wrenching words. Today it is one of the most read and respected books on the Holocaust.

After World War II, Wiesel lived in Paris, France, for 10 years where he studied at the Sorbonne and worked as a journalist, traveling to both Israel and the United States. Eventually, Wiesel moved to the United States and currently lives in New York City. In 1976, Wiesel became the Andrew Mellon Professor in the Humanities at Boston University. His book *Night* has been followed by other equally powerful books. *Against Silence: The Voice and Vision of Elie Wiesel* is a three-volume collection of his work. In 1985, Elie Wiesel was the recipient of the Congressional Gold Medal and in 1986, he was honored with one of the greatest of all awards, the Nobel Peace Prize.

Over the years, Wiesel has, in a sense, become the soul of the Holocaust. His books and lectures compel us to not only confront the issues and consequences of the Holocaust, but to keep it in our memory to ensure that history is never repeated. He lives his life, he explains, in the pursuit of meaning. Wiesel has traveled all over the world, including Bosnia, where he attempted to assist with the peace efforts. His eloquence, sensitivity, and insights serve as the voice for those who can no longer speak.

SUMMARY

Night is Elie Wiesel's personal account of the Holocaust as seen through the eyes of a 15-year-old boy. The book describes Wiesel's first encounter with prejudice and details the persecution of a people and the loss of his family. Wiesel's experiences in the death camps of Auschwitz and Buchenwald are detailed; his accounts of starvation and brutality are shattering—a vivid testimony to the consequences of evil. Throughout the book, Wiesel speaks of the struggle to survive, the fight to stay alive while retaining those qualities that make us human. While Wiesel lost his innocence and many of his beliefs, he never lost his sense of compassion nor his inherent sense of right.

kabbala: Jewish mysticism studied by Jewish scholars.

ghetto: a small area of a city to which the Jewish people were restricted and from which they were forbidden to leave.

concentration camps: a group of labor and death camps in Germany and Poland.

kapo: overseer in charge of a work detail, or some other branch of a concentration camp. Often, kapos were selected from the prisoners—usually the criminals.

PREREADING ACTIVITY The cover of *Night* contains an illustration of a lone person surrounded by barbed wire. Encourage students to study this picture and create a list of words the image brings to mind. Have students select one of the words from this class list and write a brief essay in their journals that reflects the feelings that this word evokes. Allow time for students to share their essays.

QUESTIONS AND ANSWERS

1. Why did people in Wiesel's village refuse to believe the warnings of Moshe the Beadle when he told them what happened to Jews who had been expelled from their villages in other countries? (They thought he was a madman. What he told them was too incomprehensible to be believed.)

2. Why did the people in Wiesel's village doubt Hitler's plans to exterminate the Jewish population? (They did not think it was possible to wipe out a whole people, scattered as they were throughout so many countries.)

3. How did the German soldiers win the confidence of the people of Sighet? (At first they treated the Jews politely. They lived in their homes and acted quite civilly. The people wanted to believe they were in no danger. Little by little, the soldiers took away their freedom—the leaders of the Jewish community were arrested; the Jewish people were put under house arrest; all their valuables were confiscated; the Jews were forced to wear a yellow star; the Jewish people were forced into ghettos; the ghettos were emptied and the people deported to concentration camps.)

4. At one point, upon arrival at Auschwitz, the prisoners considered revolting. What stopped them? (The older people begged their children not to do anything foolish. They still believed that they should not lose hope and must adhere to the teachings of their faith.)

5. Describe conditions in the death camps. (Prisoners were given barely enough food to survive, they were literally worked to death, they had little in the way of clothing to protect them from the freezing cold, they were kicked, beaten, and forced to suffer every inhumane treatment imaginable, and they lived with the constant threat of the furnaces.)

DISCUSSION TOPICS

1. When the Jewish people were being deported, they were allowed to take only one small bag with all their possessions. Evidence has shown that most people took their photograph albums. Why were these albums so important to them?

2. Wiesel's village was invaded by the Nazi soldiers in 1944, years after the extermination of Jews had begun. Why, after all this time, did the people have so little, if any, information about what had been happening to Jews all over Europe?

3. Wiesel was given two contrasting pieces of advice about how to survive. One was from a young Pole, a prisoner in charge of one of the prison blocks, and the other was from the head of one of the blocks at Buchenwald who spoke to Wiesel as his father lay dying. Summarize these two philosophies of survival and discuss the wisdom of each.

4. Many people ask survivors why there was so little resistance in the death camps. While there is documented evidence of some resistance in the various camps, why do you think that there were so few accounts of resistance?

5. In what ways did Wiesel's experiences affect his beliefs?

WRITING TOPICS

1. Wiesel wrote of those things he will never forget (p. 32). After reading *Night*, what images, ideas, and feelings do you think you will never forget?

2. In discussing the Holocaust, one survivor, Luba Frederick, said, "To die was easy." Based on the reading you have done, explain her statement.

3. At one point in the book, Wiesel said that he had ceased to feel human. What did he mean by this and what things can cause people to lose their sense of dignity and humanity?

4. Reread the essay you wrote in your journal for the Prereading activity based on the book's cover illustration. Revise the essay based on insights and reactions to *Night*.

5. Discuss the significance of the book's title, *Night*.

EXTENSIONS

1. Wiesel was born in Sighet in Transylvania. Locate the region of Transylvania on a pre–World War II map of Europe. Discover what happened to this area during and after World War II. Share five facts you find most significant.

2. If you could talk to one of the survivors of the Holocaust, what would you want to ask? Write to your state or local Holocaust Center (see Resources) and arrange for a survivor to speak with your class. With your classmates, determine which questions you would like the survivor to answer.

3. Create a cover for *Night* based on your own interpretations and reactions. Share your cover with classmates and explain what motivated you to create it as you did.

4. Create an "Open Letter" to those people of Europe who did little more than watch as their neighbors were persecuted.

5. Select a recurring word, phrase, or symbol from *Night*. For example, the word *night* is used frequently throughout the book. Analyze the word/ phrase/ symbol and explain the images it evokes.

...I Never Saw Another Butterfly...

Volavkova, Hana ...*I Never Saw Another Butterfly...* New York: Schocken Books, 1978.

ABOUT THE AUTHOR

...*I Never Saw Another Butterfly...* is a compilation of poems and drawings created by the children who passed through the Terezin (Theresienstadt) Concentration Camp between 1942 and 1944. The children, 15 years of age and younger, used art and poetry to convey their feelings about life, their hopes, their dreams, and their fears. The last few pages of the book include the identities of the authors and offer a few facts about each child—the year and place of birth, the number of his/her transport to Terezin and to Auschwitz, and, in most cases, the year of death.

The images created are all that remain of these children. It is their legacy to us. Of the 15,000 children who went through Terezin, only 100 survived.

SUMMARY

The Terezin (Theresienstadt) Concentration Camp, which lies approximately 37 miles from Prague, Czechoslovakia, was established as a model camp which Nazis proudly showed to foreigners who investigated the concentration camps. Also termed a ghetto, Terezin was a stopping place, a brief reprieve before victims were shipped to their deaths in the ovens and gas chambers of the concentration camps further east.

The children who came to Terezin played in the barracks and courtyard. They were allowed to work in the gardens, and even acted in plays presented for the entertainment of their guards and visitors. They were involved in poetry contests and recitations and encouraged to draw whatever they wanted. The poetry and art of the children of Terezin reflected their world. They wrote about the things they loved, the things they feared. They drew trees and flowers—symbols of life—and they drew death—the ghetto walls, the crematoriums. Their pictures and verses bring us face to face with the threat of death that they faced daily and the courage with which they faced it.

As children were transported from Terezin, they left their work with other children, who in turn, passed the pages on when they were selected to leave. The poems and drawings were finally compiled to honor the memory of these children.

Terezin (Theresienstadt): A concentration camp located outside of Prague, Czechoslovakia, that served as a model camp and a way station before victims were transported to extermination camps.

ghetto: a small area of a city into which inhabitants were crowded. Unable to escape, they lived under the most inhumane conditions, often starving to death or dying of contagious diseases.

PREREADING ACTIVITY

As an introduction to this collection of poems and pictures, read the poem "The Butterfly" aloud. Ask students, "Who do you think might have written the poem?" "To what was the poet referring?" Encourage students to react to this poem and the feelings it evoked. Introduce the book and give students some background information about Terezin (Theresienstadt) and what happened there.

QUESTIONS AND ANSWERS

1. Locate Terezin (Theresienstadt) on a map. Where is it located? Why doesn't it generally appear on maps that identify the various concentration camps throughout eastern Europe? (Terezin is located about 35 miles outside of Prague, Czechoslovakia. It was often referred to as a ghetto rather than a concentration camp.)

2. Read the epilogue to the book. How was Terezin different from other ghettos that had been established? (Terezin was a way station, a place where victims stayed just until they could be transported to one of the extermination centers. Living conditions were vastly improved in Terezin, although the victims did live under the constant threat of deportation.)

3. Why were conditions at Terezin allowed to be better than in other areas established by the Nazis for the Jewish people? (Terezin was established as a model camp. Visitors, such as members of the Red Cross, were to believe that all ghettos and concentration camps operated in a similar manner.)

4. What happened to the children of Terezin? (Of the 15,000 who were at Terezin between 1942 and 1944, only about 100 survived the Holocaust.)

5. What subjects do the majority of poems and pictures reflect? (Life and death, the struggle to survive, the knowledge of what the future holds, and the beauty beyond the walls that held them.)

DISCUSSION TOPICS

1. As you read the poems, what do they tell you about the children—their hopes, dreams, fears?

2. As you look at the pictures the children created, what do they tell you about these small victims?

3. How are the children similar to you and children you know?

4. Select one poem or picture from the book that touched an emotion in you. What comes to mind when you study it? Lead a class discussion of this work to see what additional insights can be gained from the poem/picture.

5. Why is the collection of poems and pictures such an important one?

WRITING TOPICS

1. Look through the poems. What **one word** keeps coming to mind? Write a journal entry to explain your response

2. Select one of the pictures from this book. Describe the picture so that others can see it without looking at the picture itself.

3. Reread a poem that especially touched you. Write a brief essay that explains the poem and its impact upon you.

4. Select a favorite poem/picture. What message do you wish you could send to the child who created it?

5. Think about the thousands of children who went from Terezin to their death. Imagine what contributions these children might have made to the world had they lived, and respond to the question "What might have been?"

EXTENSIONS

1. Create your own picture or poem promising the children of Terezin that they will be remembered.

2. The title poem, "The Butterfly," has been put to music and is sung in tribute to the children of the Holocaust. In small groups, select a favorite poem that could also serve as a memorial to these children. Put it to music using an existing melody or by creating your own. Teach it to others.

3. Reread the prose of Petr Fischl. Then, read his story which appears in Chapter 4 of *Memories of the Night*.

4. Obtain a copy of the video "The Last Butterfly," which tells the story of a group of children at Terezin (see Resources).

5. With others in your class, use the pictures and verses in *...I Never Saw Another Butterfly...* to create a tribute to the children of Terezin. You can do this, for example, by making slides of the art work and taping the poetry. Share the slides and accompanying tape with students in other classes.

The Children We Remember

Abells, Chana Byers. *The Children We Remember.* New York: Greenwillow Books, 1983.
Photographs from the Archives of Yad Vashem, The Holocaust Martyrs' and Heroes' Remembrance
Authority, Jerusalem, Israel.

ABOUT THE AUTHOR

Chana Byers Abells is Director of the Photo and Film Division of the Yad Vashem Archives in Jerusalem, Israel. Formerly, Ms. Abells was the Video Archivist of the Video Archive for Holocaust Testimonies at Yale University. She has edited an index of photographs covering twentieth-century European Jewry called *Archives of Destruction: A Photographic Record of the Holocaust.*

SUMMARY

The Children We Remember is dedicated to the more than one million children who were killed at the hands of the Nazis. The book, a collection of photographs from the Yad Vashem Archives in Jerusalem, is an essay about the children who lived and died during the Holocaust. Through the pictures, the events of the Holocaust unfold as seen through the eyes of these children. As we look at their faces, we are reminded again of the incredible losses and extraordinary suffering of the Holocaust—the consequence of prejudice and hate. And, in the final analysis, the pictures are a testimony to the spirit, strength, and courage of the children we will always remember.

VOCABULARY

archives: a place where public records, photographs, and other documents are kept.

child survivor: any child who was living in Nazi-occupied Europe during the years of the Holocaust whose life was significantly affected by the events of the Holocaust.

PREREADING ACTIVITY

Explain to students that approximately one and a half million children died during the Holocaust. Have students study and discuss the pictures on the front and back covers of the book. What feelings do these pictures evoke? What message do they send? Read the quote by Elie Wiesel that accompanies the picture on the back cover.

QUESTIONS AND ANSWERS

1. What was life like, in general, for the Jewish children before the Nazis took control? (Life was peaceful, the children went to school, played, prayed, and lived much like any other children.)

2. Why were the children persecuted as they were? (Because they were Jewish)

3. How did some of these children manage to survive? (Some escaped to Israel, some were rescued by Christian families, some hid in the forests, some lived as non-Jews.)

4. The pictures in this book come from the archives at Yad Vashem. What is Yad Vashem? (Yad Vashem, the Holocaust Martyrs' and Heroes' Remembrance Authority in Jerusalem, Israel, contains the world's most comprehensive collection of documentation of the Holocaust.)

5. How were the photographs in this book obtained? (Many risked their lives to document the atrocities of the Holocaust.)

DISCUSSION TOPICS

1. If one had never read, studied, or heard about the Holocaust before, what could one learn about the Holocaust from the pictures in this book alone?

2. Why is each picture considered a testimony to the Holocaust? Why are pictures like these so important?

3. Explain the significance of the last two pages of the book. Why did the author choose to end the book in a manner similar to the way in which it began?

4. How do the pictures of life before the war reflect the lives described by survivors such as Abe and Dina (Chapter 2 of this book) or others you have met through your readings?

5. Only a few of the thousands and thousands of pictures of the Holocaust are included in this book. Select one of the pictures and explain why you believe it was chosen—what is its significance?

WRITING TOPICS

1. Select one of the pictures of the children. Look at it closely for a few minutes. What does the picture say to you? What do you hear?

2. Select one of the pictures from the book. Describe what might have happened just before the picture was taken. Describe what might have happened just after the picture was taken.

3. The pictures in this book are accompanied by brief essays. Create your own essay to accompany the pictures, or create an "afterword" to the book.

4. What about the children of the Holocaust will **you** remember most?

5. Explain the phrase "Pictures are memories."

EXTENSIONS

1. What questions come to your mind as you look at these pictures? List at least five of them. In small groups, lead a discussion of two of your most interesting questions. After each person in your group has had the opportunity to lead a discussion of his/her questions, select one question from the group that generated the most thoughtful discussion and use it as the basis for class discussion.

2. The pictures in *Remember the Children* chronicle some of the major events of the Holocaust. Select one of the pictures, become involved in research to learn more about the aspect of the Holocaust it reflects, and create a one-half-page text to accompany the picture. Compile your essay along with those of others in your class to create a more in-depth text to accompany the photographs.

3. After looking at the pictures in this book, which reflect the consequences of prejudice and hate, what would you do if a racist came to speak in your community? Plan a course of action.

4. With a small group, research and read stories on the hidden children and child survivors of the Holocaust. You may also wish to write to the Child Development Research Center or to The Hidden Child Foundation, which are both child-survivor organizations (see Resource Centers in Appendix), to request stories of child survivors. Create a center in your room dedicated to child survivors and the hidden children so that others can read the information obtained.

5. The last generation of witnesses to the Holocaust are child survivors. Contact your local Holocaust Resource Center (see Appendix) to request a child survivor visit your classroom. As a class, generate a list of questions you would like your guest to address. Be certain the questions are relevant and meaningful.

PART 3

THE HOLOCAUST: LESSONS FOR TODAY

View of Majdanek Death Camp

THE HOLOCAUST: LESSONS FOR TODAY

The following projects are designed to provide you with the opportunity to apply and extend the understanding and ideas you have gained through your involvement with the history and the literature of the Holocaust.

INDEPENDENT PROJECTS

Journal Writing

Keep a journal during your study of the Holocaust. Your journal should include your reflections and feelings as well as contain your responses to the "Writing Topics" you explored in Part II. You may wish to share some of your entries with your classmates, while you might wish to keep other, more personal, reflections private.

In your journal, also keep a copy of the form on page 125, "What I Know About the Holocaust...What I Want to Know About the Holocaust... What I Discovered About the Holocaust." At the beginning of the unit, you and your classmates probably filled in the first two columns. As you continue in your study of the Holocaust, add to your list of questions in column two and in the third column answer any questions you can as well as add additional insights you have gained about the Holocaust.

A Picture—Worth a Thousand Words

Study the pictures included in *Memories of the Night: A Study of the Holocaust*. The majority of these pictures were taken on a visit to Poland, to the sites of what remains of Auschwitz, Treblinka, and Majdanek—three of the Nazi death camps. Select the picture that affects you most and react to it in some written form, such as a poem or essay. The poem on page 126 and the essays on page 127 and page vi were inspired by the collection of shoes worn by concentration camp prisoners.

Remembering the Past

George Santayana wrote, "Those who cannot remember the past are condemned to repeat it." Discuss the wisdom behind these words. Create a quotation that expresses a similar sentiment. Illustrate it and share it with your classmates.

Schindler's List

Many of you will have the opportunity to view *Schindler's List*, Stephen Spielberg's haunting movie about the Holocaust and the efforts of one man, Oskar Schindler, to save the lives of Jewish men, women, and children. After viewing *Schindler's List,* discuss the following questions:

1. Why is it important that *Schindler's List* be viewed by all people—Jews and non-Jews alike?

2. Throughout the movie, goodness and evil, living side by side, are personified. Explain this phenomenon.

3. What were your immediate feelings after viewing this movie?

4. Which scenes, in your opinion, were the most touching/distressing/important? Explain your answers.

5. Did you like Oskar Schindler? Why or why not?

6. What was the significance of the girl in the pink coat? Why did Spielberg, who used black and white film throughout most of the movie, choose to picture this little girl in pink?

7. Would Schindler consider himself to be a hero of the Holocaust? Why or why not?

8. Do you consider Schindler to be a hero of the Holocaust? Why or why not? Is there another character in the movie that you consider a hero? Explain.

9. How has *Schindler's List* affected attitudes about the Holocaust?

10. What, in your opinion, is the most important message a person should come away with after watching *Schindler's List*?

Silent Voices

During the Holocaust, "while all Jews were victims, not all victims were Jews." The Nazi government, in their zest to create the "master race," also put tens of thousands of others to death, including Gypsies and the disabled. The Nazis also murdered and brutalized African-American prisoners of war because of their race. Research these Nazi atrocities and report your findings to the class.

WHAT I KNOW...WHAT I WANT TO KNOW...WHAT I DISCOVERED

What I Know About the Holocaust	What I Want to Know About the Holocaust	What I Discovered About the Holocaust

WHERE ARE THE CHILDREN?

The shoes
All those shoes
I've never seen so many shoes

Who were they?
Where are they?
Why are they so little?
Where are the children?

Who would kill so many little children?
Who would take such innocents?
Who were in these shoes?
Who was Julika? Her name is engraved on her shoes—
For me to know her

Where is that little ballerina now?
Does she cry for her lost dancing shoe?

I can see the laces and the buckles
And the bows—

But

I can't see the children. . .

Where are they?
Who are they?
Where are the children?

Miriam Klein Kassenoff

SHOES

Even now, months later, I can still see the shoes, thread-bare, ragged, and torn. There were three rooms of shoes, rooms twelve feet high, packed from floor to ceiling with nothing but shoes. A silent memorial.

They were the shoes of those who had nothing in common and yet everything in common. They were the shoes of the young wife who would never again know a tender touch; they were the shoes of the young boy who knew nothing of play and everything about fear and survival; they were the shoes of the mother who would never sing another lullaby or hear the laughter of her children; they were the shoes of the writer, the teacher, the doctor, the dreamer.

There was a mountain of shoes reaching to forever, the shoes of the millions who lived with hope, and died still believing in tomorrow. In the end, these shoes led to one place, a place with many different names—Treblinka; Auschwitz; Birkenau; Majdanek.

I remember the shoes, and I feel a deep emptiness and an overwhelming sadness for what might have been. I wonder what roads might have been traveled, what words might have been written, what pains might have been eased. And I wonder what dreams might have come true.

Anita Meyer Meinbach

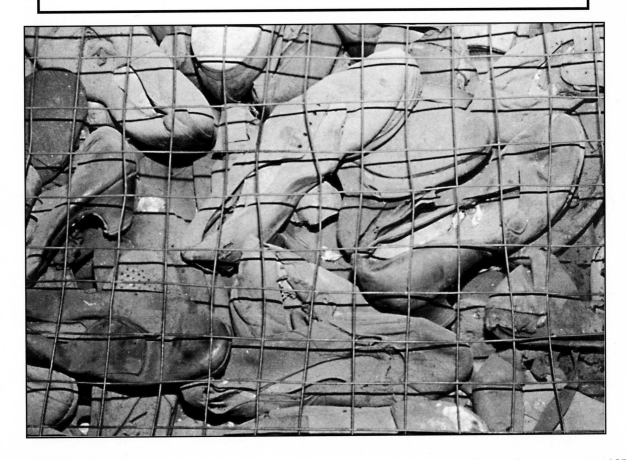

COLLABORATIVE PROJECTS

In Tribute

With a group of students, plan and prepare a tribute to one of the groups below. Your tribute might be in the form of a plaque, a statue, a song, or any other creative expression.

A tribute to the rescuers and resistance fighters of the Holocaust

A tribute to the liberators of the Holocaust

A tribute to the men, women, and children killed in the Holocaust

Artifacts Box

With others in a small group, create an Artifacts Box that captures the history of the Jewish people, a people who share a rich heritage steeped in tradition, a people almost annihilated by the Nazi regime. Be prepared to discuss the significance of the items in your box as you and your group share the contents with the rest of the class.

Peace Quilt

Think of the lessons you have learned from the Holocaust. Create a picture that in some way reflects your promise to the victims of the Holocaust that they will be remembered and that they did not die in vain. Copy this picture onto a small square of fabric, 12" x 12". Arrange your square with those of other students to form a quilt and use fabric tape to hold the squares together. Display your quilt in a prominent area of your school.

Ten Ways to Improve Multicultural Understanding

Brainstorm ways that you, your classmates, and others can help promote multicultural understanding in your school and community. (For example: invite someone from another culture to have dinner at your home; each month celebrate a different culture by preparing their foods and reading books whose main characters are members of this culture.) Compile the best suggestions into a pamphlet. Illustrate the pages and distribute the pamphlet throughout the community (banks, stores).

Visions of Peace

Create a drawing and/or writing that expresses your vision of peace. Send the class collection to children in war-torn countries to offer them hope. Contact one of the following agencies for assistance in forwarding your class collection:

American Red Cross (800-842-2200)
P. O. Box 37243
Washington, D.C. 20013

Save the Children
P. O. Box 975
Westport, CT 06881

Name _____

STAMP OUT PREJUDICE

With a partner, complete this activity sheet.

Throughout history, there have been people who have been victims of prejudice simply because of their ethnic, racial, or religious background. Choose one of the following groups (or another of your choice) as the subject of your research: Native Americans, African Americans, Jews, Mexicans, Chinese, Puerto Ricans, Haitians, etc.

1. Group you selected:_____

2. Stereotypes associated with this group: _____
   _____
   _____

3. Talk to as many members of the selected group as possible. What did you learn about the inaccuracies of these stereotypes? Explain.
   _____
   _____
   _____

4. Obtain magazine and newspaper articles that relate ways in which this group has faced prejudice. Select one article to summarize and discuss its main points with your class.

5. Complete the following questions (if necessary do additional research):
   a. How has the group you have researched experienced discrimination? Cite two examples.
   _____
   _____

   b. Identify several well-known people who are members of this group and have made significant contributions to our world. List these people and summarize their contributions:
   _____
   _____

   c. Why do you think this group has faced prejudice? Upon what is this prejudice based?
   _____
   _____

6. Develop and implement a plan of action to help "Stamp Out Prejudice" aimed at this group.

7. Create a "PEACE" stamp. Make copies of it to seal all correspondence you send as you implement your plan of action (#6 above).

8. Distribute the "PEACE" stamp to local businesses and organizations for use on their mailings as a seal (similar to the use of Easter seals).

9. Encourage your school to hold a "Stamp Out Prejudice—Peace Day" devoting all lessons and activities toward conflict resolution and peace projects.

CULMINATING ACTIVITY

HOLOCAUST REMEMBRANCE DAY

With your classmates, plan a HOLOCAUST REMEMBRANCE DAY. This should coincide with Holocaust Remembrance Week, which is usually observed in April. Contact the U.S. Holocaust Museum (100 Raoul Wallenberg Place, S.W., Washington, D.C. 20024-2150) for specific dates, materials, and other resources they provide. Invite parents, community members, your school's faculty, and students. As a class, decide what your day should include and what each student's role will be. Display time lines, posters, illustrations, diaries, and other projects created during the unit. Your day can include:

1. An introduction to the Holocaust

2. Student readings of original poems and essays

3. Dedication of the plaques, statues, etc., created in tribute to rescuers/resistance fighters, liberators, and victims of the Holocaust

4. Speeches and testimonies given by Holocaust survivors (if any live in your area)

5. Readings of specific student-made selections from the related literature of the Holocaust

6. Question-and-answer session in which questions from the audience concerning the Holocaust are addressed

7. A tree-planting ceremony during which students plant a small tree in a special area dedicated to the victims of the Holocaust as a promise of "Never Again"

8. A candle-lighting ceremony—light six candles in memory of the 6,000,000 Jewish men, women, and children of the Holocaust. As each candle is lit, one student can stand (with a survivor if possible) and state an affirmation about the future of humanity to assure others that the Holocaust will never happen again.

A FINAL NOTE TO TEACHERS:
THE HOLOCAUST IS NOT DEBATABLE

The existence of the Holocaust is not debatable. **In fact, there is more documentation of the Holocaust than of any other event in the history of humankind.** Yet, there are groups, called "revisionists," who would like to rewrite history. Students may wish to discuss the "revisionists" and their work. The best way to deal with this form of anti-Semitism is to explain to students that the motivation behind the "revisionist" tactics is prejudice and hate—their goal is to undermine everything the Jewish people have witnessed and endured. They would have us believe that there were no death camps, no gas chambers, no crematoriums, no "final solution." Remind students of the lessons of the Holocaust— to never allow themselves to be a perpetrator, a bystander, or a victim. Remind students of what happens when apathy replaces action; when tyranny replaces tolerance; and when hate replaces love.

Heather Dawn Solomon, participant in the March of the Living, April 1992.

Appendices

Time Line...134

Glossary...137

Resources...141
    Books 141
    Videos 144
    Resource Centers 147

TIME LINE

1933

Jan. 30	Hitler appointed Chancellor of Germany
Mar. 23	First concentration camp established at Dachau
Mar. 23	German parliament empowers Hitler to enact all laws on its behalf
April 1	Hitler proclaims one-day boycott of all Jewish shops/businesses
April 26	Establishment of the Gestapo
May 10	Public burning of books written by Jews and opponents of Nazism
Spring/Summer	Jewish professors are expelled from Universities; Jewish writers and artists are prohibited from pursuing their work
July 14	Nazi Party proclaimed by law to be only legal political party in Germany
Oct. 19	Germany withdraws from League of Nations

1934

Aug. 2	Hitler named president and commander in chief after death of von Hindenburg

1935

Mar. 16	Compulsory military service reinstated in Germany in violation of Treaty of Versailles
May 31	Jews barred from military service
Sept. 14	Nuremberg Laws passed depriving Jews of German citizenship

1936

Mar. 7	German Army occupies the Rhineland
June 17	Himmler appointed Chief of German Police
Oct. 25	Hitler and Mussolini form Rome-Berlin Axis
Nov. 25	Germany and Japan sign military pact

1937

July 16	Buchenwald Concentration Camp is opened

1938

Mar. 13	Germany annexes Austria
July 6	Evian Conference produces no result in helping provide refuge for Jews
Sept. 29-30	Munich Conference—England and France turn over part of Czechoslovakia to Germany
Oct. 5	Jewish passports are marked with a "J"
Oct. 28	Approximately 15,000 Polish citizens living in Germany are resettled in Poland—Poland refuses to admit them and they are stranded on the border
Nov. 9-10	Kristallnacht (Night of Broken Glass)—pogrom against Jews in Germany and Austria; Jewish shops and businesses are burned, looted, and synagogues are destroyed
Nov. 12	Jews are forced to turn over all retail businesses to Aryans
Nov. 15	Jewish students are expelled from schools in Germany
Dec. 3	Jews must hand in their drivers' licenses and car registrations
Dec. 8	Jews can no longer attend universities

1939

Jan. 30	Hitler threatens that if war erupts the Jews will be exterminated
Mar. 15	German troops invade part of Czechoslovakia
Aug. 23	Soviets and Germans sign pact of nonaggression
Sept. 1	Poland is invaded; World War II begins
Sept. 17	Soviets invade and occupy Eastern Poland
Sept. 23	Jews must turn in all radios
Nov. 28	First ghetto established in Poland—in Protrokow

1940

Feb. 12	German Jews begin to be deported to concentration camps
April 9	Germany invades Denmark and Norway
May 7	Lodz ghetto established
May 10	Germany invades Holland, Belgium, and France
May 20	Auschwitz Concentration Camp is established
June 22	France surrenders to Nazis
Nov. 15	Warsaw Ghetto is established

1941

Feb. 22	Deportation of Dutch Jews begins; Holland's workers strike in sympathy for Jews
March	Adolf Eichmann made head of Gestapo section for Jewish affairs
April 6	Germany occupies Greece and Yugoslavia
June 22	Germany invades Soviet Union
June-Dec.	Nazi Einsatzgruppen (special mobile killing units) carry out mass murder of Jews in areas of Soviet Union occupied by German Army
July 31	Heydrich appointed by Göring to carry out "Final Solution"
Sept. 1	Every Jew in areas occupied by Nazis must wear yellow Star of David
Sept. 28	Massacre of Jews at Babi Yar
Oct. 14	Large-scale deportations of Jews to concentration camps begin
Oct.	Establishment of Birkenau
Dec. 7	Japan attacks Pearl Harbor
Dec. 8	Chelmno concentration camp begins operation
Dec. 11	Germany and Italy declare war on the United States

1942

Jan. 20	Wannsee Conference—plans for "Final Solution" are made
Mar. 1	Extermination by gas begins in Sobibor
Mar. 17	Extermination by gas begins in Belzec
Mar.	Deportations to Auschwitz begin
June 1	Treblinka is established
Summer	Deportation of Jews to extermination camps from Holland, Poland, France, Belgium, Croatia; armed resistance by Jews in several ghettos
July 22	Large-scale deportation of Jews from Warsaw Ghetto
July 28	Jewish Fighting Organization (Z.O.B.) organized in Warsaw Ghetto
Oct. 4	Jews still in concentration camps in Germany to be transferred to Auschwitz for extermination

1943

Jan. 18-21	Armed Jewish resistance to Nazi attempt to liquidate Jews in Warsaw Ghetto
Feb. 2	Germany's Sixth Army surrenders at Stalingrad
March	Liquidation of Cracow Ghetto
April 19	Warsaw Ghetto revolt begins
June 11	Himmler orders liquidation of all ghettos in Poland and Soviet Union
Aug.	Revolt in Treblinka
Oct. 14	Revolt in Sobibor

1944

Mar. 19	Germany invades Hungary
May 15	Nazis begin deporting Hungarian Jews
June 6	Allied invasion of Normandy—D-Day
July 20	Attempt to assassinate Hitler fails
July 24	Russian troops liberate Majdanek death camp
Aug. 6	SS begins to drive concentration camp prisoners into Germany in advance of Soviet troops
Aug. 25	Paris is liberated
Nov.	Last deportation from Theresienstadt to Auschwitz
Nov. 8	Beginning of death march of Jews from Budapest to Austria
Nov. 24	Himmler orders destruction of Auschwitz crematoriums to hide evidence of death camps

1945

Jan. 17	Evacuation of Auschwitz—beginning of death march from there
Jan. 27	Soviet troops liberate Auschwitz/Birkenau
Feb. 4-11	Yalta Conference
April 11	American troops liberate Buchenwald
April 15	British troops liberate Bergen-Belsen
April 29	American troops liberate Dachau
April 30	Hitler is believed to have committed suicide
May 7	Germany surrenders—reign of the Third Reich is over; World War II ends in Europe
Aug. 15	Japan surrenders; World War II is over
Nov. 22	Nuremberg Trials begin

GLOSSARY

Anti-Semitism: prejudice against the Jewish people

Aryan: term used by the Nazis to describe a "race" of people they viewed as being racially superior; originally, the term used to classify an Indo-European language group

Auschwitz-Birkenau: located in Poland, largest death camp built by the Nazis; over 2,000,000 people died here by means of starvation, disease, and gassing; Birkenau is often referred to as Auschwitz II

Babi Yar: the site of a mass grave inside the Soviet border, near Kiev, where more than 100,000 Jews were shot and buried by the Nazis with the support of the Ukrainian militia

Balfour Declaration: a British government document issued in 1917 that dealt with the establishment of a Jewish homeland in Palestine

Bermuda Conference: the 1943 meeting between representatives from the United States and Britain in which the problems of refugees of Nazi persecution were discussed

Buchenwald: one of the first concentration camps; located in central Germany

Bericha: Hebrew for "flight;" name given to the organized underground assistance given to the Jews who were trying to reach Palestine after the Holocaust

Concentration Camps: work and death camps located in Germany and Poland to incarcerate and exterminate Jews, Gypsies, political dissidents, and others deemed "undesirable" by the Nazis

Crematorium: a furnace used in the death camps to cremate the bodies of victims

Dachau: one of the first concentration camps built by the Nazis, located in southwestern Germany

Death Camps: camps built to exterminate Jews and other "enemies" of the Nazi regime

Death Marches: forced marches of concentration camp prisoners as the Nazis tried to keep ahead of the Allied forces; approximately one third of those in the death marches died as a result of either disease, starvation, overexposure to the elements, or being shot by their guards

Deportation: forced removal of Jews from their homes in Nazi-occupied lands; under the pretense of resettlement, victims were sent to death and labor camps

Displaced Person Camps: camps set up after World War II as temporary living quarters for survivors of the Holocaust who now had no home or country to which they could return

Einsatzgruppen: special German mobile death squads estimated to have killed millions of Jews. Victims were executed in mass shootings and buried in unmarked graves—usually the ditches they were forced to dig

Evian Conference: conference organized by President Franklin Roosevelt and held at Evian-les-Ban in France, in 1938, to discuss the plight of Jews trying to escape Nazi persecution; 32 nations were represented but the conference did little to solve the problem

"Final Solution": Nazi code word for the physical extermination of European Jews

Gas Chamber: a sealed and airtight room where death was induced through the use of poisonous gases

Genocide: the systematic killing of a nation or race of people

Gestapo: the Nazi Secret State Police

Ghetto: an area of a city to which the Jews were restricted and from which they were forbidden to leave

Holocaust: term used to describe the systematic annihilation of the Jewish people of Eastern Europe by the Nazi regime; by the end of World War II, approximately 6,000,000 Jewish men, women, and children had been killed

Kapo: a prisoner appointed by the Nazis to oversee labor details in the concentration camps

Kovno Ghetto: one of the most well-known of the Jewish Ghettos, located in the capital of Lithuania

Gypsies: a group of people also singled out for extermination by the Nazi regime; by the end of World War II, approximately one quarter of a million Gypsies had been killed

Kristallnacht: Night of Broken Glass, the organized pogrom against Jews in Germany and Austria on November 9-10, 1938

Labor Camp: a Nazi concentration camp predominately designed for slave labor

Liberators: soldiers who freed the prisoners of the concentration camps

Majdanek: death camp located outside Lublin, one of the largest cities of Poland; most of the camp still remains today since the Nazis did not have time to dismantle it before the Russian troops arrived

Nazi: acronym for the National Socialist German Workers Party

Nuremberg Laws: issued in 1935, laws which were designed to exclude the Jews from Germany both socially and politically

Nuremberg Trials: the trial of 22 major Nazi figures held in Nuremberg, Germany, before an international military tribunal

Partisans: patriotic civilians who banned together to fight Nazi rule, usually operating in the forests in Russia, Poland, and Lithuania

Pogroms: organized acts of discrimination and violence aimed at a specific group of people

Prejudice: an attitude toward a person, group of people, or idea formed without adequate information

Racism: practice of discrimination, segregation, persecution, and domination on the basis of race

Reichstag: the central legislative body of Germany, its Parliament

Resistance: physical and spiritual opposition to the Nazi regime

"Righteous Among the Nations": the term used for non-Jews who risked their lives to save Jews from Nazi persecution

Righteous Gentiles: non-Jews who helped save Jewish lives

SA: storm troopers or Brown Shirts; organized to protect Nazi rallies

Scapegoat: an innocent person or persons blamed for the problems or troubles of another

S.D. (Sicherheitsdienst): the Security Service of the Nazi regime; headed by Reinhard Heydrich and responsible for security of the high-ranking members of the Nazi party

Shtetl: a small Jewish village in Poland

SS (Schutzstaffel): elite guard, under the command of Heinrich Himmler, responsible for the administration of the concentration camps and for carrying out the "Final Solution"

Sobibor: death camp in Poland where a quarter of a million people were gassed; setting for a famous uprising by prisoners in October 1943

Sonderkommandos: prisoners in the death camps whose jobs were to clear away the bodies of gas chamber victims

St. Louis: ship carrying Jewish refugees to Cuba and the United States in June 1939; denied safe harbor, it eventually was forced back to Europe where many of its passengers met their deaths; immortalized in the movie *Voyage of the Damned*

Swastika: symbol of the Nazi party, it was originally an ancient religious symbol

Talmud: the body of Jewish laws and prayers

Theresienstadt: Nazi ghetto located in Czechoslovakia; frequently called a "Model Ghetto" to show the outside world, including the Red Cross, how well the Jews were being treated; prisoners were kept here briefly before being transported to the death camps

Third Reich: official name of the Nazi regime; ruled from 1933 to 1945 under command of Adolf Hitler

Totalitarianism: a government or doctrine in which one political party or group maintains complete control and makes all others illegal

Treaty of Versailles: peace treaty that was signed at the end of World War I in Versailles, France; its conditions imposed economic hardships on Germany, weakened and humiliated the nation, and led to the popularity of the Nazi movement

Treblinka: one of the Nazi death camps established in Poland; between 1940 and 1943, approximately 750,000 people, many from Warsaw, were gassed there; site of a 1943 revolt in which about one-fourth of the prisoners there at the time escaped but ultimately were recaptured

Wannsee Conference: held in Wannsee, a suburb of Berlin, on January 20, 1942, to coordinate the Nazi plans for a "Final Solution"

War Refugee Board: U.S. agency established in January 1944, by order of President Roosevelt to rescue people from Nazi-occupied territories

Warsaw Ghetto (and Uprising): the largest ghetto in Europe, established in November 1940; at one time it held over 350,000 people in an area of approximately 3.5 square miles; between January and April 1943, a small group, the Jewish Fighting Organization, with few weapons, were able to hold off the Nazi soldiers; less than 100 people survived the uprising and many of them escaped to join the partisans

The White Paper: British mandate of 1939 which limited Jewish immigration to Palestine

Yellow Star: the six-pointed Star of David made of yellow cloth and sewn to the clothing of European Jews so Nazis could easily identify them

Zionism: the movement to establish a Jewish homeland in Israel

Z.O.B.: the Jewish Fighting Organization which led the uprising of the Warsaw Ghetto

Zyklon-B: the gas used in the gas chambers of the death camps

BIBLIOGRAPHY OF BOOKS AND VIDEOS

Many of the sources below were used in the preparation of *Memories of the Night*. In addition, much information comes from lecture notes taken at the Yad Vashem Seminar for Educators (1992), at the Ghetto Fighters House, Naharia, Israel (1986), and from the lecture program for the March of the Living (1992).

The U.S. Holocaust Museum in Washington, D.C., has one of the finest bibliographies of books and videos related to the Holocaust, thanks to the efforts of Dr. Helen Fagin, Chairperson of the Education Committee. For this comprehensive annotated bibliography contact:

> U.S. Holocaust Memorial Museum (202-488-0400)
> 100 Raoul Wallenberg Place, SW
> Washington, DC 20004

BOOKS:

Most of the books listed are appropriate for upper elementary school and middle school unless otherwise indicated.

History

Altshuler, David. *Hitler's War Against the Jews—the Holocaust: A Young Reader's Version of the War Against the Jews. 1933-1945 by Lucy Dawidowicz:* West Orange, NJ: Behrman House, 1978.

Arad, Yitzhak. *Ghetto in Flames.* NY: Holocaust Publications, 1982. (High School)

Bauer, Yehuda and Nili Keren. *A History of the Holocaust.* NY: Franklin Watts, 1982. (High School)

Chaikin, Miriam. *A Nightmare in History: The Holocaust. 1933-1945.* NY: Clarion, 1987.

Friedrich, Otto. *The Kingdom of Auschwitz.* NY: HarperCollins, 1994.

Gilbert, Martin. *The Holocaust: A History of the Jews in Europe During the Second World War.* NY: Henry Holt and Company, 1986. (High School)

Meltzer, Milton. *Never to Forget: The Jews of the Holocaust.* NY: Dell Publishing, 1977. (all levels)

Read, Anthony and David Fisher. *Kristallnacht: The Tragedy of the Nazi Night of Terror.* NY: Random House, 1989. (High School)

Rogasky, Barbara. *Smoke and Ashes: The Story of the Holocaust.* NY: Holiday House, 1988. (Middle School and High School)

Wild, Margaret. *Let the Celebrations Begin.* NY: Orchard, 1991. (picture book)

Resistance and Rescue

Atkinson, Linda. *In Kindling Flame: The Story of Hannah Senesh 1921-1944.* NY: William Morrow, 1992. (Middle School and High School)

Bernheim, Mark. *Father of the Orphans: The Story of Janusz Korczak.* NY: Dutton, 1989.

Bierman, John. *Righteous Gentile: The Story of Raoul Wallenberg, Missing Hero of the Holocaust.* NY: Viking, 1981. (High School)

Block, Gay and Malka Drucker. *Rescuers: Portraits of Moral Courage in the Holocaust.* NY: Holmes and Meier, 1992. (High School)

Friedman, Philip. *Their Brothers' Keepers: The Christian Heroes and Heroines Who Helped the Oppressed Escape the Nazi Terror.* NY: Anti-Defamation League, 1978. (High School)

Lifton, Betty Jean. *The King of Children: A Portrait of Janusz Korczak.* NY: Schocken, 1989. (High School)

Hilberg, Raul. *The Destruction of the European Jews.* (student text) NY: Holmes and Meier, 1985. (High School)

Meltzer, Milton. *Rescue: The Story of How Gentiles Saved Jews in the Holocaust.* NY: HarperCollins, 1991. (All levels)

Meed, Vladka. *On Both Sides of the Wall.* NY: Holocaust Publications, 1979. (High School)

Neimark, Anne. *One Man's Valor: Leo Baeck and the Holocaust.* NY: Dutton, 1986.

Nicholson, Michael and David Winner. *Raoul Wallenberg.* Ridgefield, CT: Morehouse, 1990.

Rittner, Carol and Sondra Meyers, eds. *The Courage to Care: Rescuers of Jews During the Holocaust.* NY: New York University Press, 1989. (High School)

School, Inge. *The White Rose: Munich, 1942–43.* Hanover, NH: University Press of New England, 1983. (High School)

Schur, Maxine. *Hannah Szenes: A Song of Light.* Philadelphia: Jewish Publication Society, 1986. (Middle School and High School)

Stadtler, Bea. *The Holocaust: A History of Courage and Resistance.* West Orange, NJ: Behrman House, 1975. (all levels)

Vinke, Hermann. *The Short Life of Sophie Scholl.* NY: Harper and Row, 1980.(High School)

Voices of the Holocaust: Biography/ Personal Accounts

Appleman-Jurman, Alicia. *Alicia: My Story.* NY: Bantam, 1988. (Middle School and High School)

Auerbacher, Inge. *I Am a Star: Child of the Holocaust.* NY: Prentice Hall, 1987. (for younger readers)

Frank, Anne. *The Diary of a Young Girl.* NY: Doubleday, 1967. (Middle School and High School)

Gies, Miep. *Anne Frank Remembered: The Story of the Woman Who Helped to Hide the Frank Family.* NY: Simon and Schuster, 1988. (High School)

Isaacman, Clara and Joan Grossman. *Clara's Story.* Philadelphia: Jewish Publication Society, 1984.

Leitner, Isabella. *Fragments of Isabella: A Memoir of Auschwitz.* NY: Dell, 1983. (High School)

Levi, Primo. *Survival in Auschwitz.* NY: Macmillan, 1987. (High School)

Reiss, Johanna. *The Upstairs Room.* NY: HarperCollins, 1990.

Roth-Hano, Renee. *Touch Wood: A Girlhood in Occupied France.* NY: Puffin Books, 1989.

Sender, Ruth. *The Cage.* NY: Macmillan, 1986.

Tec, Nechama. *Dry Tears: The Story of a Lost Childhood.* NY: Oxford University Press, 1984. (High School)

Toll, Nelly. *Behind the Secret Window: A Memoir of a Hidden Childhood During World War II.* NY: Dial Books, 1993. (Middle School and High School)

Van der Rol, Ruud and Rian Verhoeven. *Anne Frank: Beyond the Diary.* NY: Viking, 1993. (Middle School and High School)

Wiesel, Elie. *Night.* NY: Bantam, 1982. (Middle School and High School)

Zar, Rose. *In the Mouth of the Wolf.* Philadelphia: Jewish Publication Society, 1983.

Poetry/Art/Photographs

Abells, Chana Byers. *The Children We Remember.* NY: Greenwillow, 1983. (all levels)

Blatter, Janet and Sybil Milton, eds. *Art of the Holocaust.* NY: Rutledge Press, 1981. (High School)

Bernbaum, Israel. *My Brother's Keeper: The Holocaust Through the Eyes of an Artist.* NY: Putnam, 1985.

Toll, Nelly. *Without Surrender: Art of the Holocaust.* Philadelphia: Running Press, 1978. (all levels)

Szner, Zvi and Alexander Sened, eds. *With a Camera in the Ghetto.* NY: Schocken, 1987. (Middle School and High School)

Volavkova, Hana, ed. *I Never Saw Another Butterfly: Children's Drawings and Poems from Terezin Concentration Camp 1942-1944.* NY: Schocken, 1993. (all levels)

Historical Fiction

Applefeld, Aharon. *To the Land of the Cattails.* NY: Weidenfeld and Nicolson, 1986. (High School)

Bunting, Eve. *Terrible Things: An Allegory of the Holocaust.* Philadelphia: Jewish Publication Society, 1989. (all levels)

Gehrts, Barbara, *Don't Say a Word.* NY: Macmillan, 1986.

Innocenti, Roberto. *Rose Blanche.* NY: Steward Tabori and Chang, 1991. (picture book)

Laird, Christa. *Shadow of the Wall.* NY: Greenwillow, 1990.

Lustig, Arnold. *Darkness Casts No Shadows.* Evanston, IL: Northwestern University Press, 1985. (High School)

Lowry, Lois. *Number the Stars.* Boston: Houghton Mifflin, 1989.

Matas, Carol. *Daniel's Story.* NY: Scholastic, 1993.

Matas, Carol. *Lisa's War.* NY: Charles Scribner's Sons, 1989.

Orlev, Uri. *The Island on Bird Street.* Boston: Houghton Mifflin, 1981. (all levels)

Ozick, Cynthia. *The Shawl.* NY: Random House, 1990. (High School)

Richter, Hans. *Friedrich.* NY: Puffin, 1987.

Yolen, Jan. *The Devil's Arithmetic.* NY: Viking, 1988.

TEACHER RESOURCE BOOKS/ADULT BOOKS

History

Arad, Yitzhak, Yisrael Gutman and Abraham Margaliot, eds. *Documents on the Holocaust: Selected Sources on the Destruction of the Jews of Germany and Austria, Poland, and the Soviet Union.* Yad Vashem: KTAV Publishing House, 1981.

Bauer, Yehuda and Nili Keren. *A History of the Holocaust.* NY: Franklin Watts, 1982.

Berenbaum, Michael. *The World Must Know: A History of the Holocaust as Told in the United States Holocaust Memorial Museum.* Boston: Little Brown, 1993.

Chamberlin, Brewster and Marcia Feldman, eds. *The Liberation of the Nazi Concentration Camps, 1945: Eyewitness Accounts of the Liberators.* Washington, DC: Government Printing Office for the U.S. Holocaust Memorial Council.

Dawidowicz, Lucy. *The War Against the Jews 1933-1945.* NY: Bantam, 1986.

Dawidowicz, Lucy. *A Holocaust Reader.* West Orange, NJ: Behrman House, 1976.

Dwork, Deborah. *Children With a Star: Jewish Youth in Nazi Europe.* New Haven, CT: Yale University Press, 1991.

Epstein, Helen. *Children of the Holocaust.* NY: Viking Penguin, 1988.

Friedlander, Albert. *Out of the Whirlwind.* NY: Schocken, 1989. (anthology arranged by themes)

Gilbert, Martin. *The Macmillan Atlas of the Holocaust.* NY: Macmillan, 1982.

Gilbert, Martin. *The Holocaust: A History of the Jews in Europe During the Second World War.* NY: Henry Holt and Company, 1986.

Hilberg, Raul. *The Destruction of the European Jews.* (3 volumes). NY: Holmes and Meier, 1985.

Lipstadt, Deborah. *Denying the Holocaust: The Growing Assault of Truth and Memory.* NY: The Free Press, 1993.

Langer, Lawrence. *Holocaust Testimonies: The Ruins of Memory.* New Haven, CT: Yale University Press, 1991.

Lanzmann, Claude. *Shoah: An Oral History of the Holocaust.* NY: Pantheon, 1987.

Levin, Nora. *The Holocaust: The Nazi Destruction of European Jewry, 1933-1945.* Melbourne, FL: Krieger Publishing, 1990.

Marrus, Michael. *The Holocaust in History.* NY: New American Library/Dutton, 1989.

Shamir, Ilana. *The Young Reader's Encyclopedia of Jewish History.* NY: Viking, 1987.

Wyman, David S. *The Abandonment of the Jews.* NY: Pantheon, 1986.

Yahil, Leni. *The Holocaust: The Fate of European Jewry, 1932-1945.* NY: Oxford, 1991.

Resistance and Rescue

Keneally, Thomas. *Schindler's List.* NY: Simon and Schuster, 1992.

Meed, Vladka. *On Both Sides of the Wall.* NY: Holocaust Publications, 1979.

Tec, Nechama. *Defiance: The Bielski Partisans. (The Story of the Largest Armed Rescue of Jews by Jews during World War II).* NY: Oxford University Press, 1993.

Tec, Nechama. *When Light Pierced the Darkness: Christian Rescue of Jews in Nazi Occupied Poland.* NY: Oxford University Press, 1987.

Voices of the Holocaust: Biographies and Personal Accounts

Kosinski, Jerzy. *The Painted Bird.* NY: Random House, 1983.

Leitner, Isabella. *Fragments of Isabella: A Memoir of Auschwitz.* NY: Dell, 1983.

Levi, Primo. *Survival in Auschwitz.* NY: Macmillan, 1987.

Nir, Yehuda. *The Lost Childhood.* San Diego: HBJ, 1991.

Ozick, Cynthia. *The Shawl.* NY: Random House, 1990.

Ringelblum, Emmanuel. *Notes From the Warsaw Ghetto: The Journal of Emmanuel Ringelblum.* New York: Schocken, 1974.

Wiesel, Elie. *The Town Beyond the Wall.* NY: Schocken, 1982.

Poetry, Art, and Photographs

Blatter, Janet and Sybil Milton, eds. *Art of the Holocaust.* NY: Rutledge Press, 1981.
Hinz, Bertold. *Art in the Third Reich.* NY: Pantheon, 1979.

TEACHER GUIDES

Rossell, Seymour. *The Holocaust, The World and the Jews, 1933-1945.* West Orange, NJ: Behrman House, 1992.
Shawn, Karen. *The End of Innocence: Anne Frank and the Holocaust.* NY: Anti-Defamation League, 1989.

VIDEOS

Addresses and phone numbers of all video companies/suppliers are listed after the video references. Videos are recommended for Middle School and High School unless otherwise indicated.

Auschwitz: If You Cried You Died.
Subject: Chronicle of two survivors retelling the horrors and their experiences at Auschwitz
Impact America Productions, Inc.

Children in the Holocaust
Subject: Examines the plight of Jewish children in the Holocaust, from the viewpoint of those children, now adults
Grades: Senior High to Adult
Phoenix/BFA Films and Video

The Courage to Care
Subject: Reminds viewers of the difference each individual makes in following his/her conscience
Zenger Video

Daniel's Story
Subject: Events of the Holocaust are told from a child's perspective
Grades: 3-8
U.S. Holocaust Memorial Museum

Dear Kitty
Subject: Tells the life of Anne Frank
Anne Frank Center

Genocide, 1941-1945 (A World at War Series)
Subject: The destruction of the Jews in Europe is shown through archival footage and testimonies of victims, perpetrators, and bystanders
A & E

Flight From Destiny
Subject: Interview with survivors of the SS *St. Louis*
Video Archive for Holocaust Testimonies at Yale

The Hangman
Subject: Animated version of poem by Maurice Ogden in which people are mysteriously hanged, one by one, while the townspeople stand by and watch
CRM

The Holocaust: Turning Point Series
Subject: Traces the Nazi Regime's efforts to annihilate the Jewish People
Grades: High School
CRM

Image Before My Eyes
Subject: Recreates Jewish life in Poland from the late nineteenth century to the time of the Holocaust
Simon Wiesenthal Center

Korczak
Subject: The true story of a doctor and the 200 orphans he cared for in the Warsaw Ghetto
New York Films Video

Lodz Ghetto
Subject: History of one of the last ghettos to be liquidated
Jewish Heritage Project, Inc.

The Last Sea
Subject: The exodus of Jews from Europe to Israel after World War II ended
Ergo Media, Inc.

March of the Living, 1992
Subject: Documents the visit of thousands of Jewish teens from all over the world as they visit major death camps of Poland in May 1992.
Available from: US. Office of the March of the Living
110 E. 59 St., 3rd Floor
New York, NY 10022

The Only Way
Subject: The story of one Jewish family and the people of Denmark who helped them
Social Studies School Service

Persecuted and Forgotten
Subject: Account of the extermination of the Gypsies during the Holocaust
EBS Productions

Raoul Wallenberg: Between the Lines
Subject: The story of Raoul Wallenberg, the Swedish diplomat, who saved thousands of lives during the Holocaust and whose ultimate disappearance remains a mystery
Grades: High School
Social Studies School Services

Survivors Among Us
Subject: Excerpts from testimonies of survivors living in Boston
Video Archive for Holocaust Testimonies at Yale

Triumph of the Will
Subject: Propaganda film made for the Nazis
Zenger Video

Triumph of Memory
Subject: Non-Jewish resistance fighters tell of the atrocities in the death camps
PBS Video

Through the Eyes of a Friend
Subject: Tells the story of Anne Frank; addresses stereotypes, prejudice, and discrimination
Living Voices

The Upstairs Room
Subject: True story of Annie de Leeuw, as she and her sister survive World War II in hiding
Grades: 4-9
Social Studies School Service

Voices of Survival
Subject: Personal recollections of the Holocaust
Suncoast Media, Inc.

The Wannsee Conference
Subject: Tells of the conference in which leading Nazis discussed plans for the "Final Solution"
Zenger Video

The Warsaw Ghetto
Subject: Documentary of the most well-known of the ghettos established by the Nazis; includes life in the ghetto and the resistance in its final weeks
Zenger Video

World War II: The Propaganda Battle
Subject: Bill Moyers' examination of how propaganda and media were used during World War II to affect public perceptions
PBS Videos

Additional Videos—available through most local video stores
Diary of Anne Frank
Escape from Sobibor
Europa, Europa
Judgment at Nuremberg
The Nasty Girl
Playing for Time

Sources of Videos
A & E Home Video (800-423-1212)
P.O. Box 2284
South Burlington, VT 05407

Anne Frank Center (212-529-9532)
106 East 19 St.
New York, NY 10003

CRM (800-421-0833)
2215 Faraday, Suite F
Carlsbad, CA 92008

EBS Productions (415-495-2327)
330 Ritch Street
San Francisco, CA 94107

Ergo Media, Inc. (800-695-3746)
P.O. Box 2037
Teaneck, NJ 07666

Impact America Foundations, Inc. (317-848-5134)
1900 Keystone Crossing, Suite 390
Indianapolis, IN 46240

Jewish Heritage Project, Inc. (212-925-9067)
150 Franklin St., #1 W
New York, NY 10003

Living Voices (206-328-0798)
915 East Pine
Suite 405
Seattle, WA 98122

New York Films Video (212-247-6110)
16 W. 61 St.
New York, NY 10023

PBS Videos (800-344-3337)
1320 Braddock Pl.
Alexandria, VA 22314

Phoenix/BFA Films and Video (314-569-0211)
2349 Chaffee Dr.
St. Louis, MO 63146

Simon Wiesenthal Center (310-553-9036)
9760 W. Pico Blvd.
Yeshiva University of Los Angeles
Los Angeles, CA 90035

Social Studies School Services (800-421-4246)
10200 Jefferson Blvd., Room J.
P.O. Box 802
Culver City, CA 90232

Suncoast Media, Inc. (800-899-1008)
2938 West Bay Dr., Suite B
Belleair Bluffs, FL 34640

U.S. Holocaust Memorial Museum (202-488-0400)
100 Raoul Wallenberg Pl. SW
Washington, DC 20004
Contact them for a comprehensive annotated list of videography.

Video Archive for Holocaust Testimonies at Yale (203-436-2157)
Sterling Memorial Library, Room 331 C
Yale University
New Haven, CT 06520

Zenger Video (800-421-4246)
10200 Jefferson Blvd, Rm. 902
P.O. Box 802
Culver City, CA 90232

HOLOCAUST RESOURCE CENTERS

The following institutions provide resources and information:

U.S. Holocaust Memorial Museum
100 Raoul Wallenberg Place, S.W.
Washington, D.C. 20004
(202-488-0400)

American Gathering and Federation
of Jewish Holocaust Survivors
122 West 30th Street
Suite 205
New York, NY 10001
(212-239-4230)

Anne Frank Institute of Philadelphia
437 Chestnut Street
Lafayette Building, Suite 221
Philadelphia, PA 19106
(215-625-0411)

The Child Development Research
(International Study of Organized Persecution of
Children)
30 Soundview Lane
Sands Point, NY 11050
(516-883-7135)

Association of Holocaust Organizations
Dallas Memorial Center for Holocaust
7900 Northhaven Rd.
Dallas, TX 75230
(214-750-4654)

Facing History and Ourselves National Foundation
25 Kennard Rd.
Brookline, MA 02146
(617-232-1595)

Gratz College Holocaust Oral History Archive
10th and Tabor Rd.
Philadelphia, PA 19141
(215-329-3363)

The Hidden Child Foundation
Anti-Defamation League of B'nai B'rith
823 United Nations Plaza
New York, NY 10017
(212-490-2525)

Holocaust Documentation and Education Center
Florida International University
N.E. 151 Street and Biscayne Blvd.
North Miami, FL 33181
(305-940-5690)

Holocaust Education and Memorial Center of Toronto
4600 Bathurst St.
Willowdale, Ontario, M 2-R 3V2
Canada
(416-635-2883)

Holocaust Memorial Resource and Educational Center
of Central Florida
851 North Maitland Ave.
Maitland, FL 32751
(305-628-0555)

Holocaust Resource Center Archives—Queensborough
Community College
Queensborough Community College
Bayside, NY 11364
(718-225-1617)

International Center for Holocaust Studies—
Anti-Defamation League of B'nai B'rith
823 United Nations Plaza
New York, NY 10017
(212-490-2525)

International Network of Children of Holocaust
Survivors
Florida International University
N.E. 151 St. and Biscayne Blvd.
North Miami, FL 33181
(305-940-5690)

Jewish Labor Committee
25 E. 21 St.
New York, NY 10010
(212-477-0707)

Leo Baeck Institute
129 East 73 Street
New York, NY 10021
(212-744-6400)

Martyrs Memorial and Museum of the Holocaust
6505 Wilshire Blvd.
Los Angeles, CA 90048
(213-852-1234)

The National Catholic Center for Holocaust Education
Holocaust Education-Seton Hill College
Seton Hill Drive
Greensburg, PA 15601
(412-834-2200, ext. 344)

New York Holocaust Memorial Commission
342 Madison Ave.
Suit 717
New York, NY 10017
(212-687-5020)

Simon Wiesenthal Center
9760 West Pico Blvd.
Yeshiva University of Los Angeles
Los Angeles, CA 90035
(212-553-9036)

Video Archive for Holocaust Testimonies at Yale
Sterling Memorial Library Yale University
Room 331 C
New Haven, CT 06520
(203-432-1880)

Warsaw Ghetto Resistance Organization
122 West 30 St.
New York, NY 10001
(212-564-1065)

International Resources:

Ghetto Fighters House
Naharia, Israel

Yad Vashem
Education Department
Jerusalem, Israel